MIKAL KEEFER

GROWING
SPIRITUAL GRIT

FOREWORD BY **RICK LAWRENCE**

52 PERSONAL DEVOTIONS

JESUS-CENTERED DEVOTIONS

Group | L I F E T R E E®

Growing Spiritual Grit
52 Personal Devotions

Lifetree™ is an imprint of Group Publishing, Inc.

Visit our website: group.com

Credits
Author: Mikal Keefer

Chief Creative Officer: Joani Schultz

Senior Editor: Candace McMahan

Assistant Editor: Cherie Shifflett

Art Director and Designer: Jeff Storm

Production Artist: Andy Towler

Unless otherwise indicated, all Scripture quotations are taken from the Holy Bible, New Living Translation, copyright © 1996, 2004, 2007, 2013, 2015 by Tyndale House Foundation. Used by permission of Tyndale House Publishers, Inc., Carol Stream, Illinois 60188. All rights reserved.

ISBN: 978-1-4707-5338-2 (hardcover), 978-1-4707-5545-4 (ePub)

Printed in China.

10 9 8 7 6 5 4 3 2 1   27 26 25 24 23 22 21 20 19 18

CONTENTS

FOREWORD

Does your desk look like mine?

I mean, is it a chaotic mess punctuated by piles of bills, projects, and rubber-banded correspondence waiting for you to pay attention?

From 15 feet away, these piles look like square-ish icebergs floating on the sea of my desktop, crashing into each other and covering 97 percent of the surface area.

Unlike icebergs, though, my piles are noisy—they cry out to me with the shrill blast of a screaming toddler...

- *You thought you were going to scrape by on the bills this month, but you forgot this one, didn't you? What will you do? I asked, WHAT WILL YOU DO?*

- *Umm...Weren't you supposed to make that appointment for a yearly physical exam? I wonder what undiscovered health concerns lurk in you, right now, because you've avoided this so long...*

- *What about those forms you were supposed to fill out for your daughter's college financial aid—have you missed the deadline?*

- *And what exactly are those yellowing pages at the bottom of that pile on the right side of your desk? Talk about procrastination—something under there must be pretty intimidating...*

The screaming toddlers of our everyday pressures, responsibilities, and challenges can wear us out. Maybe that's why we crave our favorite escape hatches (food, drink, entertainment) just to forget about our troubles for a micro-season.

But that won't put a cork in the toddler's mouth—it's all waiting for us on that desk or in that email inbox.

We need strength and perseverance to travel through the rough terrain of life. But along the way, we discover that our own strength and perseverance are often not enough.

We need something bigger and tougher. We need grit.

Grit is the engine that drives perseverance. It's the core strength that helps us face and overcome challenges and obstacles. And it's the essential characteristic that sustains our lifelong journey with Jesus.

Without grit, our faith wavers, distractions derail us, and our focus blurs.

And here's the kicker: Every person of great impact in the world, everyone who has lived out the mission and work of Jesus in world-changing ways, needed grit to do it. In fact, these people needed a supercharged version of grit that is stronger than the garden-variety stuff we've all developed along the way.

That "regular" version helps us hang tough when we're tempted to quit, and it helps us solve difficult problems that seem too big to overcome. But personal grit is limited by our capabilities; *spiritual* grit is fed by the limitless resources of Jesus and is anchored by a growing dependence on him.

When we are captured by a passion for Jesus, we're motivated to point our little dinghy toward that sea of icebergs with a determination that is beyond our own capacity.

Not only do we take on the tough stuff, but we discover joy in the journey because Jesus is our intimate companion.

In his letter to the followers of Jesus living in Rome, the Apostle Paul describes the mechanics of spiritual grit: "We can rejoice, too, when we run into problems and trials, for we know that they help us develop endurance. And endurance develops strength of character, and character strengthens our confident hope of salvation. And this hope will not lead to disappointment. For we know how dearly God loves us, because he has given us the Holy Spirit to fill our hearts with his love" (Romans 5:3-5).

With the "dear love" of God sustaining us, we find the grit we need to not merely slog through our challenges but to actually "rejoice...when we run into problems and trials." That's a crazy-miraculous way to live. And it's available to everyone, no matter how big our icebergs appear to be.

And speaking of miracles, my friend Mikal Keefer performed one with the book you're holding right now.

He immersed himself in my book *Spiritual Grit*, soaking his hyper-creative brain in its pages, and then created this companion devotional that is uniquely and brilliantly practical.

In the thoughts and questions and ideas you're about to encounter, you'll find a path toward transformation in your life. If you feel stuck in your personal trajectory or long for greater strength in the midst of challenges or want to help the people you love grow in their own core strength, you're going to love this book.

And as daunting as all of this might sound, you're going to be shocked by how fun the journey is.

Rick Lawrence
Author of *Spiritual Grit*

INTRODUCTION

You know those devotional books you read first thing in the morning, snuggled in a comfy chair with a mug of coffee steaming at your elbow?

This isn't one of those.

These are devotions you can't do in your pajamas—at least, not most of them.

They're not about making you comfortable.

If anything, they'll make you a bit *uncomfortable*—because they'll have you doing the very things Jesus had his first followers do. Hard things, but things that ultimately gave those disciples the fortitude to own their faith, stand strong, and follow Jesus no matter what.

These devotions will help you grow grit. *Spiritual* grit.

Grit is that elusive quality that enables people to persevere, to commit, and stay committed. It's what propels some people forward when they're too exhausted to take another step. It's dedication—but it's something more.

Grit picks up where dedication leaves off. It's what gives the very best athletes their edge, what pushes some people to hammer away at an injustice long after everyone else has walked away.

And *spiritual* grit is what keeps some people tightly focused on and abiding in Jesus, following him no matter how difficult the path. It's rare, powerful, and transformative.

And it's exactly what Jesus is looking to build in you.

Here's the catch: You develop spiritual grit much as you develop grit anywhere else in your life: by doing stuff.

Hard stuff.

Hard stuff that turns out to be good for you. That helps you rely on Jesus and see him working in and through you.

Hard = Good, at least in the kingdom of God.

We call these 52 grit-growing devotions "*do*-votions" because each asks you to *do* something.

To move just outside your comfort zone, out to where you can see Jesus more clearly. To have conversations you've not had before, to look at people through fresh eyes, to lean into challenging things.

To risk relying on Jesus.

You get two options in each devotion: to do something gritty and to do something even grittier. Feel free to do one or both. Ask Jesus what he recommends.

You'll then reflect on what you've experienced and talk it over with Jesus. That's a grit-builder, too.

And you'll find brief accounts of how other people—people like you—have grown grit in their lives. It's an opportunity to tag along as they discover the same lessons you'll discover in your own life.

Because after all, we're all in this grit thing together.

Don't worry; there's nothing here that will leave scars. But you *will* stretch—in a good way. In a spiritually gritty way.

So take a deep breath...and let's get started.

Let's grow a little grit.

KEEP THE FAITH—
AND TRUST JESUS

It's several years into Jesus' ministry, and the disciples can see the wheels are falling off.

The crowds have thinned. Religious leaders Jesus has offended along the way are circling around like wolves closing in for the kill.

And Jesus seems unable—or maybe unwilling—to do anything about it. Even after he's publicly criticized. Even after a crowd in the Temple courtyard tries to stone him to death.

Even as the disciples point out the obvious: Jerusalem is no place for Jesus—or them. They'll be walking into a lions' den the moment they cross back into Judea.

But Jesus isn't persuaded. He's going to Judea and on into Jerusalem with or without them.

So it's up to the disciples to decide: Do they trust Jesus enough to follow him when everything they see tells them to cut their losses and walk away?

There's no question that they believe in Jesus, that they have faith. The miracles they've seen, the teaching they've heard, the healings that made Jesus famous—all of that convinced them long ago that he is who he says he is.

But when their lives are on the line, do they trust him?

Thomas' response to the dilemma is classic. He draws in a long, deep breath and then sighs, "Let's go, too—and die with Jesus" (John 11:16).

Then this band of brothers, this dozen disciples, silently falls into step behind Jesus.*

Jesus' first disciples don't just have faith in Jesus—they trust him. And faith and trust are less alike than they appear at first glance.

Having faith actually isn't all that hard.

You can easily have faith that an ancient elevator creaking open in front of you is safe. It's carried passengers for decades, it was installed back when things were built to last, and some inspector has signed off that the floor's solid and the cables aren't frayed.

But when you step into the elevator and punch a button for the 30th floor, that's when faith turns into trust.

Faith prompts a nod of agreement. Trust prompts action.

If that's true—if trust translates into something that can be seen, heard, touched—what can you point to in your life that indicates you trust Jesus?

Read the entire account in John 11:1-16.

GRIT GROWER I: TRUST WALK

You may be more trusting than you think.

Not sure about that?

Do this: Walk around your house or apartment and briefly touch everything you trust, often without even being aware you trust it.

That medicine bottle on the kitchen sink: You trust that the pharmacist didn't accidentally substitute cyanide.

The electric outlet? You trust it will work when you plug in the vacuum cleaner.

The TV or tablet on which you watch news? You trust that what you see on it is the truth, nothing but the truth and...well, maybe you don't trust *everything* in your house.

And that's okay: It's wise to trust carefully.

See how many objects—or people—you touch in a five-minute trust walk.

And Even Grittier

Take a virtual hike through the contact list on your phone. How much do you trust the people whose names scroll past?

Who's trustworthy? mostly trustworthy? less trustworthy?

And how do you decide where each name falls on your trust scale?

Now consider this: If Jesus did this same exercise and your name scrolled past, how do you think he'd rank your name on his list of trustworthiness? Why?

What did you discover about yourself and trust?

_____

_____

What did you discover about Jesus?

_____

_____

What—if anything—would Jesus have to say or do to increase your trust in him?

_____

_____

Where was the spiritual grit in these experiences? You've now grown as a result of what you've done. What's different about you now, and why?

_____

_____

GRIT GROWER 2: TRUSTING FOR THE RIGHT WORDS

There's a reason we love coming up with plans and then asking Jesus to put his stamp of approval on them: It means we're in control.

Which isn't all that trusting. Or grit-growing. Or God-honoring.

So do this: Pick up your phone. Ask Jesus who he'd have you call—and why.

It could be someone who needs to feel remembered. Or maybe it's someone whose relationship with you is strained. It could be someone you've never met.

Listen for Jesus' voice. Be open to a face floating into focus.

Trust that what comes to mind was prompted by Jesus...and make the call.

And Even Grittier

It's time for a field trip.

If possible, take another Jesus-follower with you so you can talk about the experience afterward. But if that doesn't work, it's no problem.

You won't be alone.

Go to the nearest hospital emergency room, and when you get to the door, pray this: "Jesus, for the next hour, I'm at your disposal. You lead, and I'll follow."

Then walk in, find a seat in the waiting area, and trust that Jesus will tell you what's next.

Maybe he'll ask you to pray for that woman weeping in the corner. Or strike up a conversation with the angry man pacing the room.

Trust Jesus for direction. For the right words. For whatever's coming next.

• ⋯⋯⋯⋯⋯⋯⋯⋯⋯⋯⋯⋯⋯⋯⋯⋯⋯⋯⋯⋯⋯⋯ •

What did you discover about yourself through these experiences?

_____

_____

What did you discover about trusting Jesus?

_____

_____

In what ways does putting yourself out there without a plan build your trust in Jesus?

_____

_____

Where was the spiritual grit in these experiences? How are you different as a result of these experiences, and why?

_____

_____

GRIT GROWER 3: TELL A SECRET

And not just any secret.

Tell a *secret* secret—one that would complicate your life if it were whispered around. That would scuttle your ship if it were posted to social media.

The sort of secret you've walled off inside yourself. That you haven't shared with many people…maybe with anyone, ever.

A secret that's a weight, a chain around your heart.

Find a place where you can speak out loud and not be heard. Then share that secret with Jesus. Hear yourself say it aloud.

Picture his face as he listens to you. What's that you see in his eyes?

And Even Grittier

Tell that same secret to a person—a person you trust.

Who? That's up to you, but beware: You're putting your comfort, perhaps even your future, in that person's hands.

So choose wisely.

What's the secret? And who's the person?

What did you discover about yourself through these experiences?

_____

_____

What did you discover about trusting others?

_____

_____

How trusting would you say your relationship with Jesus is? Why do you answer as you do?

_____

_____

Where was the spiritual grit in these experiences? What strength have you gained through them?

_____

_____

SPIRITUAL GRIT MEETS...
A MEDICAL TRAGEDY

When Lynne met Chris, she couldn't believe her luck.

"We were a perfect fit," she says. "I loved being outdoors, and he felt the same. We worked in the same industry. We both loved God—and still do."

A quick courtship; a wedding crowded with friends and family; and then a honeymoon of lazy mornings, afternoon hikes in the mountains, and biking through some of the most spectacular scenery on the planet.

Where, on a remote trail, Chris' mountain bike caught a rock, flipping him over the handlebars.

And snapping his neck.

Chris survived, but as a quadriplegic. In a split second, Lynne's and Chris' lives changed forever. And in one way, they changed for the better.

"I discovered I was married to a prayer warrior," says Lynne. "There was so much he couldn't do any longer, but he could pray—so that's what he did. Constantly. For me, for other people, for the world at large.

"Chris and God became best friends."

Another unexpected outcome of Chris' situation was that both he and Lynne found they had no choice but to trust Jesus.

For income.

For Chris' ongoing health.

For their relationship to survive now that much of their physical intimacy was gone.

No, they're not living the life they imagined—and they'll be the first to tell you that. They've long ago tossed out the window any expectations and assumptions about how their life together would unfold.

There have been significant, profound losses. More than once they've looked at their lives and wondered what God had in mind when he placed them where they are. They've wondered when and how Chris will finally get comfortable with his view from a wheelchair.

From the outside, relying on their own understanding, this tragedy makes no sense.

But Lynne and Chris are thriving because they're also trusting.

Which means they're pretty sure the word *tragedy* doesn't really describe what happened.

If God's in it, it's not a tragedy. If Jesus is somehow expressing his love and drawing them closer to him through what's happened, no matter how painful it is, they'd be fools not to embrace him even in their discomfort.

"We aren't doing this on our own," says Lynne. "We lean on Jesus. We turn to him around the clock. We look for the Spirit in every situation.

"And above all, we trust that Jesus knows what he's doing."

Spiritual grit: to have a default setting of trust in Jesus when inexplicably hard things happen, to come to him for help rather than to lay blame at his feet.

What's your default setting when hard things happen?

Is it trust…or something else?

LOVE YOUR ENEMIES— ALL OF THEM

Now and then Jesus says something that makes his disciples miserable.

For instance, imagine how they feel when they hear this:

"You have heard the law that says, 'Love your neighbor and hate your enemy.'

"But I say, love your enemies! Pray for those who persecute you! In that way, you will be acting as true children of your Father in heaven.

"For he gives his sunlight to both the evil and the good, and he sends rain on the just and the unjust alike.

"If you love only those who love you, what reward is there for that? Even corrupt tax collectors do that much. If you are kind only to your friends, how are you different from anyone else? Even pagans do that.

"But you are to be perfect, even as your Father in heaven is perfect" (Matthew 5:43-48).

Jesus' disciples trade a few uncomfortable glances when they hear those words. They've been traveling together, and you know how guys talk—they've been sharing stories about who's on their naughty and nice lists.

And they *have* been praying about their enemies—but not the way Jesus commands. They've been praying more about enemies getting hit with lightning than blessings.*

To want the best for people who've hurt you? That's gritty.

To actively seek *good* for those enemies? Back up the wheelbarrow—that's a whole big *pile* of grit.

Clearly, as far as enemies are concerned, the first disciples are in need of an attitude adjustment...and they're not alone.

Jesus calls his followers—including you—to love others as God loves you. To pass along what you've received. To actively seek what's best for others even if they don't acknowledge or appreciate it.

Hard? Try impossible, at least on your own.

It takes grace. And if you've tried living gracefully, you know that's nothing you can pull off on your own.

But here's the good news: You're *not* on your own. You're following Jesus, and he's in this with you.

Grace is powered by Jesus himself; it's his fingerprints on the world. When you experience grace—on either the giving or receiving end—you know Jesus can't be far away.

When's the last time you spotted Jesus' fingerprints on your life?

Read the entire account in Matthew 5:31-48.

GRIT GROWER 4: MAKE AN ENEMIES LIST

First, let's get this on the table: You have enemies.

Maybe no one's shooting at you or paying an assassin to poison your pasta, but there are people who don't wish you well. Or who ignore you.

That woman at work who seems intent on torpedoing your career.

The neighbor whose dog barks all night and, when you complain, dismisses you with a "deal with it" shrug.

Or perhaps someone damaged you years ago, but the wounds still sting. What happened may be in the past but, so far, you're not past it.

Your enemy is anyone who's hurt you, whether deliberately or by willful indifference. Anyone on that list—everyone on it—is who Jesus expects you to love.

Not just tolerate.

Even if you buy the Hard = Good equation, that's a tough sell. But you don't have a choice. Jesus isn't requesting your attendance at the Love Your Enemy Ball; he's telling you to do your level best to get there.

Do this: List your enemies on a sheet of paper. List anyone who has hurt you or is hurting you now, anyone whose indifference causes you pain.

Post the list where you'll see it often.

Then, at the top of that list, write this: My Prayer List.

Start praying, and see what happens in your world...and in you.

And Even Grittier

Share your list with another Jesus-follower. Ask that person to pray for you as you pray for the people on your list.

And—if you're really going for grit—invite your friend to ask you now and then how it's going.

How you're being transformed.

How you're becoming more like Jesus.

What did you discover about yourself through these experiences?

What did you learn about Jesus?

When you started praying, what if anything happened in your world...or in you?

Where was the spiritual grit in these experiences? What strength do you have that you didn't have before?

_____

_____

GRIT GROWER 5: ENGAGE THE ENEMY

Maybe you've noticed: Things are tense these days.

Civil conversations about volatile issues are rare. And listening with the intent of understanding another person's point of view—that's pretty much on the endangered species list.

Which means it's easier than ever to make enemies and demonize anyone who disagrees with you.

Do this: Think of an issue you're passionate about. It might be political, or it could be a moral stance you hold dear.

Whatever the issue, find an acquaintance on the other side of the fence and say: "I wonder if you'd help me understand why you see things the way you do?"

Come with a sincere desire to understand, not debate. To accept, even if you don't endorse what you hear.

And then listen until the person who's speaking feels understood.

Perhaps even loved.

And Even Grittier

Select a *family member* who's on the other side of an issue, someone with whom you've sparred in the past.

Maybe it's atheist Uncle Jasper or the brother who thinks carrying a bazooka down Main Street is his God-given right. Any family member who holds an uncompromising point of view that differs from yours is fair game.

Ask Jesus to use this experience to reframe what might be a contentious relationship with your family member.

And ask him for the grit to stay engaged in the conversation.

What did you discover about yourself through these listening experiences?

_____

_____

In what ways did your feelings about your "enemy" shift during your conversation...or didn't that happen?

_____

_____

Where was the spiritual grit in these experiences? In what ways do you feel stronger?

_____

_____

GRIT GROWER 6: INSTITUTIONS ARE PEOPLE, TOO

Of course you'd never hate an individual. You're far too kind for that.

But how about your phone company or internet provider? The DMV? Or some brick-for-brains politician who seems intent on driving your county, state, or country off a cliff?

What about the institutions on which you've declared war? The ones you trash on social media and kick through the mud whenever you talk about them?

They can be enemies, too.

If you're following Jesus, you'll treat institutions the same way he treated the Roman army that he knew would one day spike his hands and run a spear through his side.

So here's a grit-building suggestion: Call your least-favorite institution's customer service line and tell whoever answers about something they've done *right*.

Don't complain; compliment.
Love your enemy.

And Even Grittier

Call a company that you've already trashed, and apologize.

Tell whoever answers the phone what you did, and ask for forgiveness.

Trust me: This will be the only time the service representative on the other end will have *that* happen.

You'll be the talk of the break room.

•···•

What did you discover about yourself through these experiences?

_____

_____

What did you discover about loving your enemies?

_____

_____

In what ways was what you did hard...and good?

_____

_____

Where was the spiritual grit in these experiences?

_____

_____

_____

Sometimes the events that turn someone into your enemy aren't all the fault of your enemy.

Sometimes you contribute, too.

And if that's the case, here's a grit-growing recommendation from Jesus:

"So if you are presenting a sacrifice at the altar in the Temple and you suddenly remember that someone has something against you, leave your sacrifice there at the altar. Go and be reconciled to that person. Then come and offer your sacrifice to God" (Matthew 5:23-24).

Actually, it's less a recommendation than an order.

To the extent you can make what's wrong between you and another person right, make it right.

Look at the prayer list (see Grit Grower 4), and pick a name. What, if anything, did you contribute to negatively affecting that relationship? And what, if anything, might you do to help fix what's broken?

Would an apology help? a more concrete action?

If you broke it, fix it. At least try.

And Even Grittier

Some say Jesus was just making a point when he said to settle differences before coming before God in worship. Others think he meant exactly what he said.

There's great grit in taking him literally on this one.

Before you show up at church or a Bible study again—before you finish this do-votion—reach out to someone you've hurt and take a step toward making it right.

Meter's running.

What did you discover about yourself through these experiences?

_____

_____

What did you discover about Jesus?

_____

_____

In what ways was this experience hard...and good?

_____

_____

Where was the spiritual grit in these experiences? In what way do you feel freer than before?

_____

_____

SPIRITUAL GRIT MEETS...
THE ENEMY

When Chuck's supervisor introduced him to the new guy, it was obvious the new employee wasn't just new to the warehouse where Chuck worked.

He was also new to the United States.

And Chuck, a Vietnam veteran who came home with enough hard memories to last a lifetime, knew precisely where Bao was from: Vietnam.

"I needed more back story before I could get on board with being around this guy, let alone making him feel welcome," Chuck says.

Fortunately, Bao's back story did the trick.

Bao was a political refugee from Vietnam, a soldier who'd fled the country before South Vietnam fell. That reassured Chuck; he and Bao had been on the same side, they'd been brothers in arms.

"The guy was great," Chuck says. "He showed up early, stayed late, and worked so fast that he made the rest of us look bad by comparison. We couldn't ask for a better worker."

Chuck wonders now why it never occurred to him to ask why Bao had been forced to leave South Vietnam when the communists took over. There had been thousands of South Vietnamese soldiers, and they didn't all qualify as political refugees. What had been so special about Bao?

When Chuck found out, he was floored.

Yes, Bao had fought for South Vietnam. But before that, before he'd defected, he'd served in the NVA—the North Vietnamese Army. Had he been discovered in Vietnam at the end of the war, he'd have been executed on the spot by the North Vietnamese.

No wonder he'd had to escape.

"The guy working next to me had literally been my enemy," says Chuck. "If I'd met him when I was in Vietnam, I'd have killed him without a second thought."

Except Bao wasn't just another VC. He was Bao—a man Chuck had come to know and respect…even admire.

Standing next to him, day after day, was the enemy. But not the enemy.

Standing next to him, if Chuck wanted, was a friend.

It was Chuck's decision—and a gritty one at that. One that called for a grace-laced blend of forgiveness and compassion.

"Love your enemies" suddenly became more than something Jesus said to Chuck; it became something Jesus expected of him.

Jesus expects it of you, as well.

SERVE OTHERS

Jesus is the hottest ticket in town.

He walks into view, and multitudes gather. Some come to be healed, some for a free meal, and others just to watch the show.

But they show up by the thousands. And when they do, the disciples are by Jesus' side, basking in the applause and adulation that wash over Jesus.

For James and John, two professional fishermen accustomed to long, lonely nights on the water, it's an energizing experience.

They feel the crush of the crowds. They see people point toward them, recognizing them as insiders in the Jesus extravaganza.

It's heady stuff, and James and John enjoy it, perhaps a bit too much.

When their mother asks Jesus to give her boys favored spots in whatever new government he's creating, Jesus sees straight through her. He knows she's asking because her sons put her up to it.

What follows is a humbling, grit-building experience for James and John.

After telling them it's the Father's decision who'll be at his side, Jesus uses their request as a launching pad for a lesson on humility and servanthood.

Earthly rulers may lord their power over others, but that's not how things work in the kingdom of God. In Jesus' world, new rules apply.

"Whoever wants to be a leader among you must be your servant," Jesus says. "And whoever wants to be first among you must become your slave" (Matthew 20:26-27).

Gritty words, and hard to hear for anyone grasping for position and power in Jesus' outfit. Both are available, Jesus says, but you won't get them by demanding them. And if you do end up at his side, many of the benefits most leaders enjoy will be missing.

You won't be served. You'll be serving others.

You won't be first in line. You'll be last.

And then there's this: There's no room for whining because Jesus is doing the same thing you're doing: serving others.

"For even the Son of Man came not to be served but to serve others and give his life as a ransom for many," Jesus says (Matthew 20:28).

Notice that Jesus doesn't call out James and John and humiliate them. He knows all his disciples are wondering the same thing: *How can I benefit from knowing Jesus? What's in it for me?*

Those are very human questions, ones you've likely considered a time or two.

What's in it for you? The answers are the same now as they were then: purpose, passion, and eternal life. Good stuff comes from loving and serving Jesus. It's just not the stuff that puts new cars in your garage or builds a shiny résumé.

And every one of those benefits comes wrapped in this: servanthood.

Servanthood is the gravel pit of grit—it's humbling, hard, relentless, and all but impossible.

Ask any mother about meeting the overwhelming, all-consuming needs of her new baby. The center of her life shifts; she's no longer nearly as concerned about her own comfort as she is about caring for her baby.

What keeps her going is love (and the occasional nap).

What keeps Jesus' followers serving others is also love—love for those they serve and the One they follow. Any other motivation quickly wears thin.

Here's one way to know you're following Jesus: Your path is marked by opportunities to serve others.

How many of those opportunities are you seeing in your life?

And who are you serving?

We ask, not to shame you, but simply to raise the questions. Friends (can we call you a friend?) do that for each other: They ask prickly questions and have hard conversations because those are also ways to serve others.

So pause to consider your answers. They'll help you know if you're following Jesus or simply your notion of who Jesus might be.

What opportunities to serve are you seeing in your life?

And who are you serving?

Read the entire account in Matthew 20:20-28.

GRIT GROWER 8: BAG IT AND TAG IT

Find a heavy-duty trash bag and a pair of work gloves.

All set?

Good—you're about to spend an hour serving people who aren't likely to thank you. And that's a hard-but-good thing for sure.

Some won't notice what you're doing.

Others will notice but won't care.

Either way, don't count on anyone aiming an appreciative "thumbs-up" your way as you stroll through the neighborhood picking up trash that's settled on sidewalks, blown into doorways, and otherwise landed where nobody's likely to clean it up.

Which is what you're about to do.

A question to think about as you fill your bag with broken glass, discarded cans, and stray scraps of who-knows-what: How does it feel to serve when nobody appreciates you or your efforts?

Instead of striving to be appreciated, look inward to Jesus. What is *he* saying to you?

And Even Grittier

Ratchet up your service: Adopt the route you just walked and do this again next week...and the week after.

See if this act of service becomes a habit.

See if anyone joins you.

And don't worry if nobody does.

What did you discover about yourself through these experiences?

_____

_____

How is what you've just done like or unlike what Jesus did as well?

_____

_____

In what ways was this experience hard...and good?

_____

_____

Where was the spiritual grit in these experiences? How has your "core strength" grown through these experiences?

_____

_____

GRIT GROWER 9: HELP GRANDMA

Okay, not necessarily her.

But get ready to serve *someone* in your family—someone you can help in 15 minutes or less.

Maybe it's stepping in to do a chore that's on your child's list, not yours. Quickly cleaning the kitchen because your spouse dearly loves an uncluttered countertop.

Or giving Mom a foot rub. Dad a neck rub. Or maybe calling Grandma for a how-are-you-doing chat.

Ask Jesus who in your family would be encouraged by 15 minutes of selfless service and what that service might be.

While you're at it, ask him this, too: How have you been serving me in ways I haven't noticed or appreciated? Listen for his voice. Then thank him.

And Even Grittier

Make the same offer to an elderly or infirm neighbor. Offer to do an hour of whatever needs to be done.

Be clear this isn't a request for a job; there's no invoice coming.

If there's something on your neighbor's list you can't do (plumbing comes to mind), talk with other neighbors and recruit some help.

Serve...with no expectation of payment.

Serve as Jesus serves you.

As the calluses form on your fingers, you'll feel grit growing in your heart.

What did you discover about yourself from these service experiences?

What did you discover about Jesus?

In what ways was this experience hard...and good?

Where was the spiritual grit in these experiences? What did you do that required Jesus' strength to do, and why?

This might get tricky.

Pick the right building, and you'll grow grit on a public sidewalk. Pick the wrong one, and you'll grow some grit in the back of a police car.

So...choose wisely.

Dress nicely; then go to a much visited public building—a library, government office building, or shopping mall. Just be sure it doesn't have doors that open automatically.

Position yourself so you can easily open the door for people coming in and out. Appoint yourself temporary doorman and perform the two essential doorman duties: Open the door and smile graciously as you do so.

Don't require a response, but do make eye contact and silently pray for each person you assist.

If asked what you think you're doing, simply say, "I wanted to serve today."

Oh, and a note: Don't try to do valet parking. That's called grand theft auto.

And Even Grittier

Open other kinds of doors.

Open a door to a relationship with someone who's lonely by inviting that person into your life. Create a welcoming space where a friendship might flourish.

Open a door to mentoring someone who's a few steps behind you on her career path.

Open a door by intentionally serving as a bridge between people you know who'd enjoy knowing each other. Introduce them.

Open doors and then step back and watch Jesus use what you've done.

By the way, extra points if you're an introvert.

What did you discover about yourself as you served others?

_____

_____

How is what you did like or unlike what Jesus did—and does?

_____

_____

In what ways was this experience hard...and good?

_____

_____

Where was the spiritual grit in these experiences? What was one unexpected outcome you've enjoyed because of these experiences?

_____

_____

GRIT GROWER 11: LOOK FOR SOMEONE WHO'S STRUGGLING

This grit-building experience couldn't get much simpler. It involves looking and then serving.

In the Bible's description of Jesus' ministry, he's always pausing to help someone. Run out of wine at a wedding celebration? Jesus helps out. Leprosy issue? Jesus to the rescue. Want to sort out a tricky theological issue? Jesus has your back.

Do the same today: Notice someone who's struggling and offer to help.

Maybe someone at work could use a word of encouragement.

Or down the street, someone may be struggling to clear a yard of leaves or a sidewalk of snow.

A person at the grocery store may be juggling way too many items and could use a helping hand or two.

Look around you today.

Look...notice...and serve.

And Even Grittier

Look deeper. Who's sad? Who's feeling the ache of loss? Who has fear etched on his face?

Serve by asking, "How are you? How are you *really*?"

Then listen...for as long as it takes.

•••

What did you discover about yourself as you looked and served?

_____

_____

How was your serving like Jesus' expectations of his first disciples?

_____

_____

In what ways was this experience hard...and good?

_____

_____

Where was the spiritual grit in these experiences? Jesus said that when we serve "the least of these" we have actually served him. How does that truth affect the way you serve?

_____

_____

SPIRITUAL GRIT MEETS...
A CRAWL SPACE

The next time you're in Amsterdam, stroll over to 263 Prinsengracht, about a 20-minute walk from the train station.

That's where you'll find the Anne Frank House. A museum now fills the tall brick building that hid Anne's family during the Nazi occupation in World War II.

Hid them until August 4, 1944, that is, when German police stormed up the stairs to arrest everyone hiding in the attic.

Anne Frank's story has been told in the international best-seller *The Diary of Anne Frank.*

But there's another story on this street, one behind the front door of a row house just a few steps from the museum.

"My great-aunt lived there during the war," says Brent, who grew up hearing about and from his elderly Dutch relative. "That's what I've been told, at least. What I know for certain is that she, too, lived nearby—and she sheltered Jews."

Brent's Aunt Tessa let a Jewish husband, wife, their children, and their governess live in a crawl space in her home. If they'd been discovered, Tessa would have been arrested and hanged.

But unlike the Franks, the family sheltered by Tessa was never discovered. Her hidden guests lived undetected for years, depending on Tessa to somehow find enough food to feed not only her family but theirs as well.

It was a tense life lived in tight quarters, punctuated by terror as first the Germans and then the Allies took Amsterdam by force.

When at last Amsterdam was liberated in May of 1945, Jews who'd survived in hiding were free to at last walk into the sunlight.

For the first time in years, they could breathe fresh air. Feel the spring breeze on their skin. And do more than pace the floor in claustrophobic closets and crawl spaces.

"The family whose lives my aunt saved waited until the Germans surrendered before doing anything more than peeking from between closed curtains," says Brent.

"But once the coast was clear, they were up and out of the house as quickly as possible.

"They left without saying goodbye or offering Tessa so much as a 'thank you.' They simply…walked away. She never heard from them again."

Tessa didn't harbor any ill feelings toward the people she'd served. She'd set out to save them. That's what she accomplished.

And that's what spiritual grit looks like: It doesn't serve to earn applause or gratitude. It serves because serving reflects the heart of Jesus.

Jesus "came not to be served but to serve others and to give his life as a ransom for many" (Matthew 20:28).

That's who you're following…and that's the gritty path he'll lead you down.

The other teachers weren't sure if they should congratulate Nicole or turn her over to Child Services.

It could have gone either way.

During a series of lessons on helping others, Nicole brought a goldfish to her first-grade classroom and left it up to her students to care for it.

"Naming it, feeding it, changing the fishbowl water, finding Goldie a home for the holidays and summer—all of it," says Nicole. "I bought a tube of food and left it next to the bowl, but that was all."

The idea was to serve up a hefty dose of real-world consequences for her kids to experience if they failed to serve the fish. So Nicole left Goldie's fate in the hands of 28 kids who were far more concerned about soccer and socializing than goldfish maintenance.

"I told the kids that if they failed to help and serve Goldie, she'd die," says Nicole.

A few kids took it on themselves to assure Goldie's survival, but soon their interest faltered.

Goldie's bowl grew cloudy. Some days she got too little food and other days too much. On the weekends if nobody had gotten the okay from a parent to haul Goldie home, the fish gutted it out on her own.

And then, one morning, kids bounced into their room to find Goldie glassy-eyed and floating upside down.

"She was one dead goldfish," says Nicole, who gathered the kids around Goldie's bowl for a discussion about how helping Goldie might have kept her healthy. About how, if they'd looked, they'd have known she needed help.

That's the part that some of the other teachers didn't like. And one parent thought it a bit more real-world than her daughter deserved to hear.

But Nicole also pointed out that, if kids look, they can see when people need help, too. And they can choose to serve those people.

"Nobody had any problem with that part of my message," Nicole remembers.

It was a powerful day, and one that transformed Nicole's classroom.

"Kids started looking out for one another," says Nicole. "And the next month, when I brought a hamster in, he was treated like royalty. Kids made a schedule and took turns cleaning, cuddling, and feeding him—they didn't miss a day.

"They'd learned the cost of not caring for the classroom pet with Goldie, and the lesson stuck.

"I'm pretty sure Hector the Hamster is still there," says Nicole, who moved to another school the following year. "He's never going to graduate to second grade."

Something hard sparked compassion in Nicole's class, and the grit kids grew by losing Goldie helped them not to lose sight of one another.

How has the grit grown in one corner of your life bled into other parts of your life? How is your spiritual grit showing itself in how you regard yourself or others?

EXPECT THE UNEXPECTED

A crowd has hiked into the wilderness to see Jesus. Thousands of people have dropped everything to see him.

Unfortunately, one thing they dropped was a quick trip home to gather up picnic supplies to carry with them.

Now they're here, dinnertime is fast approaching, and the disciples have pulled Jesus aside to suggest he send people away so the crowd can find food.

In response Jesus says, "*You* feed them."

Then he goes back to what he was doing: healing, teaching, and most definitely *not* sending people away.

So...now what? Because *that* was totally unexpected.

Yes, Jesus has given his dozen closest disciples the ability to cast out demons and heal illnesses, but rustling up dinner for more than 5,000 people? They have no idea where to begin.

There isn't enough money to buy food, and even if they had cash, where would they go? There's not a bakery in Israel that can bag up enough bagels to satisfy the throng surrounding Jesus.

But Jesus is expecting them to do *something*...

The Gospel writer John notes that it's Andrew who finds the young man who's carrying five barley loaves and two small fish. What John doesn't describe is *how* Andrew knows the kid's packing a snack.

Is it possible that, even though there's no hope they'll collect enough food, the disciples fan out to ask for donations? And this youngster is the only one dumb enough to raise his hand and risk losing what little he has?

The answer is yes.

Yes, it's completely possible because that's exactly what you might have tried—you and anyone else who wants to please Jesus but doesn't know how to begin to accomplish an impossible task.

In whatever way the young man was outed, he's hustled straight to Jesus.

You know what happens next: Jesus miraculously multiplies the meal until there's enough fish sandwiches for everyone—with 12 baskets of leftovers to haul home.*

Jesus could have made things easier for his disciples. He could have simply prayed a catered lunch into existence—but that's not what he chooses to do.

Instead, he hands them a how-do-I-solve-this challenge and tells them to act. When they do, he multiplies and blesses what they accomplish, no matter how meager the fruit of their labors.

And that's how grit grows. Jesus asks, we do, and then we see what he does with the little we bring to him.

And an annoyingly large percentage of Jesus' requests come as surprises.

Someone with whom you have a fractured relationship ends up behind you in line at the grocery store, and you've no excuse for not talking. You come into a sudden pile of unexpected money (hey, it could happen), and you're forced to decide: Spend it on yourself or others?

If you're following Jesus, expect the unexpected. It's coming. It's how he rolls.

Yes, Jesus could have solved the disciples' problem for them, but grit doesn't grow on the path of least resistance or easy answers.

For them, for you, it's found far more often where there's no choice but to do your best and turn to Jesus for help.

*Read the entire account in Matthew 14:13-21.

GRIT GROWER 12: TEMPORARY LEFTY...OR RIGHTY

Sometimes it's easier to see Jesus when you step outside your routines, even a little.

Do this: Get ready for your day using your nondominant hand. If you're a righty, brush your teeth with your left hand.

Lefty? Button and zip up your clothes with your right hand.

Allow extra time, by the way; tying your shoes is going to take some doing.

As you feel your patience grow thin, as you struggle with tasks you can usually do on automatic pilot, notice the unexpected— maybe unwelcome—surprises that show up.

Ask yourself: In what ways is what you're experiencing like following Jesus?

And how do you typically react to the challenging surprises he tosses your way?

And Even Grittier

It's hard to plan your own surprises, so you'll need some help.

Call a friend and ask for her help with a quick project at your house or apartment. Twenty minutes, tops.

When your friend arrives, ask her to rearrange your living room furniture. She's to move every stick of furniture somehow. Drag the sofa over here, place the lamp over there—you get the idea.

Meanwhile, you'll wait in another room as your friend redecorates.

Live with the new furniture placement for at least a week. See how long it takes you to get accustomed to what was a *substantial* surprise when you first walked into the room.

A word of advice: Leave a lamp burning at night. Should you walk through the room in the dark, your shins will get a sharp reminder that the coffee table has migrated.

What did you discover about yourself as you coped with surprises?

_____

_____

How was this like what the first disciples experienced in their lives?

_____

_____

In what ways was this experience hard...and good?

_____

_____

Where was the spiritual grit in these experiences? In what ways have you depended more on Jesus as a result of these surprises?

_____

_____

GRIT GROWER 13: EAT WHAT SHOWS UP

Not every surprise is welcomed with open arms.

When they involve a dozen friends leaping out and screaming "Surprise!" as they smother you with hugs and happiness, that's one thing.

When surprises come in the form of frozen pipes, unexpected bills, and stray aches and pains, they're greeted with considerably less enthusiasm.

But you can learn plenty from any surprise...including this one.

Go to a sit-down restaurant, and when the server asks what you'd like to order, provide a price range and a list of any food allergies. That's it. Explain you'd like the server to decide.

Whatever it is, assuming you can afford it and it won't send you into allergy-related shock, you'll eat it.

As you eat the...well, whatever is set before you...be mindful that this is _exactly_ the sort of gritty surprise Jesus loves tossing at you: something nourishing if not quite to your taste.

Welcome to discipleship.

And Even Grittier

Forget the cost, and don't even glance at the menu.

Tell your server that you're ordering the fourth entrée listed, the fifth side dish, and the third drink.

Get ready for a surprise.

What did you discover about yourself through one or both of these experiences?

_____

_____

As you reflected on surprises Jesus has let come your way, what did you discover about him?

_____

_____

In what ways was this experience hard...and good?

_____

_____

Where was the spiritual grit in these experiences? What's one practical way you can invite more surprise into your life?

_____

_____

GRIT GROWER 14: THAT OTHER CHANNEL

You have approximately 300 channels available on your television and a bazillion more on your laptop or tablet, but you probably watch fewer than a dozen with any regularity.

Not today.

Pick a channel at random—one you never select—and watch for half an hour. Expose yourself to something new and surprising (but not something you have to repent of later). Look for anything that reminds you of Jesus.

You'll be surprised what leaps out at you.

Surprise!

And Even Grittier

Call that friend from the "Even Grittier" section of Grit Grower 12 and explain you'd like to take her to the movies.

Your treat...sort of.

Pick a time, and together, head to the local multiplex. When you get to the box office, buy tickets to the next movie that's showing—even if you've never heard of it. Even if you've heard of it and thought, "There's no way I'd sit through *that*."

Buy two tickets, hand one to your brave friend, and rustle up a bucket of popcorn to share.

Then find two seats and settle in.

Afterward, go somewhere the two of you can talk about the film and how this was like dealing with surprises that pop up in life. How sometimes doing unexpected things gets you ready for other unexpected things. How grit is worth growing.

You're going to have a *great* conversation.

•···•

What did you discover about yourself as you went through these experiences?

_____

_____

How was this like dealing with surprises that Jesus lets come into your life—especially those that show up because you're following him?

_____

_____

In what ways was this experience hard...and good?

_____

_____

Where was the spiritual grit in these experiences? How does inviting risk into your relationship with Jesus draw you closer to him?

_____

_____

OBEY JESUS

Obedience.

There's a word not likely to be voted Most Likely to Succeed.

Anyone who's lived with a 2-year-old knows we're wired for anything *but* obedience. We all have opinions we want noted, preferences we expect to be respected.

And whether or not we say it aloud, we're pretty sure our way is the best way.

Jesus' first disciples were a lot like us in that regard, so it's likely they were less than thrilled when Jesus said, "If you love me, obey my commandments" (John 14:15).*

Just…obey, no questions asked?

Meaning Jesus won't put all major decisions to a vote?

Really?

Jesus sets obedience as a quick, no-compromise bar he expects anyone following him to clear.

Um…just who does this Jesus character think he *is*?

And there—right there—is the heart of the matter.

Jesus can demand obedience precisely *because* of who he is: Savior. Lord. Master. God.

He doesn't owe anyone a rationale or explanation. He doesn't have to cajole or convince. He's in charge; the kingdom of God isn't a democracy.

His followers don't get a vote; they just get to decide if they love him.

If they love him, they'll follow him.

And if they follow him, they'll obey.

This is gritty stuff made all the grittier because we tend to hear the word *obey* as a harsh command. It's what annoyed parents say to disobedient children. It's all about establishing who's in charge.

But Jesus doesn't insist on obedience just to flex his muscles. He's ever and always about love. He obeys the Father (John 6:38) because of love, and he expects you and the rest of his followers to obey him for the same reason.

Because you love him.

For Jesus, obedience is all about the heart, not just behavior.

So maybe *obey* isn't a four-letter word after all. At least, not a distasteful one.

Jesus' expectation of obedience is an opportunity rather than a mean-spirited demand.

An opportunity to reap the benefits of abiding in him.

An opportunity to have an even closer friendship with him.

An opportunity to grow grit.

*Read the entire account in John 14:15-21.

GRIT GROWER 15: OBEY THE RULES

Make that obey *all* the rules—including the ones you usually ignore. Even the dumb rules that make no sense to you.

Driving? Stay under every posted speed limit. Stop fully at every stop sign. Toss your cellphone in the trunk so you won't be tempted to check for emails.

Working? Make sure your 15-minute break doesn't stretch a second longer. Fill out the forms in triplicate. Fill the drawers of the photocopy machine.

Writing a report? Check your grammar and spelling as if your life depended on it. Not sure whether it's supposed to be a colon or a semicolon? Check with someone who knows.

Clean up after yourself. Wash your hands when the health department expects you to. Stick to your diet. Read all the instructions before beginning.

In short, become a poster child for the Keep the Rules Foundation.

All the rules. All day. No exceptions.

And Even Grittier

Disobey all the rules—and see what happens.

See how far you get today before your life gets very, very complicated.

Ask yourself as you go: Which is the better way to care for myself and others: through obedience or disobedience?

How does each stance affect your relationship with Jesus?

•···•

What did you discover about yourself as you explored obedience?

_____

_____

How was your attitude toward obeying *all* the rules like or unlike your attitude toward obeying Jesus?

_____

_____

In what ways was this experience hard...and good?

_____

_____

Where was the spiritual grit in these experiences? How might Jesus use them as you move forward in your journey with him?

_____

_____

Rustle up a $20 bill, and carry it with you this week.

Tell Jesus you understand it's his money and you're just hauling it around.

Then ask Jesus what he wants you to do with his money. Tell him if he'll let you know, you'll do it.

That's the deal: He speaks, you obey. Even if you don't fully understand or even agree with what he says.

Here's a chance for you to practice hearing Jesus' voice. And to respond, not with reluctance but with enthusiasm.

And Even Grittier

Make it a $100 bill.

Because having a stray $100 bill tucked in your pocket will definitely move this do-votion to the front of your mind, that's why.

Listen for Jesus' voice...and do as he asks.

With the $100 bill, certainly—but also with the rest of your life.

•••

What did you discover about yourself as you went through these experiences?

_____

_____

What was it like expecting Jesus to speak to you? And how did it turn out? What did you hear? Or didn't you hear anything?

_____

_____

In what ways was this experience hard...and good?

_____

_____

Where was the spiritual grit in these experiences? Why do challenges that involve money have such a big impact on us?

_____

_____

GRIT GROWER 17: TAKE AN ORDER

Give yourself an assignment. Order yourself to bake a cake... change your car's oil...get that nasty stain out of the carpet.

Anything that you have no idea how to do.

Now find a how-to online tutorial, and figure out how to obey the order you gave yourself.

As you charge into unknown territory, you're obeying—but it's energizing, isn't it? Even if you fail, you're fully engaged, alive, and focused.

How is that like obeying Jesus?

And Even Grittier

You're going to need to borrow an old dog.

A friendly one.

Your goal: to train an old dog to do a new trick. It can be roll over, play dead, or drive a stick shift—whatever you decide.

Just be sure the dog doesn't already know the trick. That's cheating.

Use whatever treats and techniques you think will best convince the dog to listen to you and obey the command.

Give yourself an hour; then see how the dog performs.

It doesn't count if the dog intends to obey but doesn't get around to it. Or if Fido explains that what you've asked isn't convenient or in his area of giftedness.

The dog either will or won't obey your command.

It will happen...or it won't.

So give this a try...and as you do, ask yourself this: In what ways is what you're doing like and unlike what Jesus does with you?

And in what ways are you like or unlike Fido?

•···•

What did you discover about yourself as you went through these experiences? And how about the dog—did the dog learn anything?

_____

_____

What did you discover about obedience and how Jesus goes about helping you obey him?

_____

_____

In what ways was this experience hard...and good?

_____

_____

Where was the spiritual grit in these experiences? We often say that if we knew exactly what Jesus wanted us to do, we'd do it, but that's often not true. Why do we disobey even when we know what Jesus wants?

_____

_____

Go to a river, lake, or pond where you can toss rocks into the water without creating a problem.

(Swimming pools are out. Let's get that straight at the get-go.)

Take a pocketful of pebbles or pennies with you. Anything you can toss in the water and not miss later.

As you stand next to the water, think of ways you haven't obeyed Jesus.

Things you've done. Things you've left undone. Things you've said or thought. With each memory of a disobedient moment, toss one of your pebbles into the water and watch it disappear from sight.

This may take awhile.

When you've finished—or run out of pebbles—tell Jesus you're sorry. Ask for his help as you move forward in your gritty, stop-and-start discipleship journey.

You've just repented, and Jesus is faithful to forgive, so let those memories of disobedience disappear under the water just as the pebbles did.

Instead of looking over your shoulder, look ahead.

At a life of transformation. Of growing in your friendship with Jesus. Of obedience, not because you have to but because you want to honor your friend.

And Even Grittier

Add a second pocketful of pebbles and repeat this activity—this time choosing to forgive the people who've disobeyed you.

Children who deliberately lied to you. Colleagues who dropped the ball and left you holding a problem instead of a completed project. Friends whose follow-through left you disappointed.

Forgive their disobedience as Jesus has forgiven yours.

What did you discover about yourself as you considered those times you and others have been less than obedient?

_____

_____

How did it feel to confess...and repent...and be forgiven?

_____

_____

In what ways was this experience hard...and good?

_____

_____

Where was the spiritual grit in these experiences? Why do we require so much strength to be humble and vulnerable?

_____

_____

SPIRITUAL GRIT MEETS...
THE COACH

When Daryl was offered a college basketball scholarship, nobody was more surprised than Daryl.

"I was a mediocre player," he recalls. But the small college recruiting him couldn't tap top talent, so Daryl got a call and took the offer. He was heading off to college to play ball and feeling pretty puffed up about it.

Temporarily.

The bubble burst when Daryl's coach handed him a summer training schedule. One that included precisely zero time playing basketball.

The coach actually *forbade* Daryl to touch a basketball throughout the summer.

"He said no one on the team was all that talented and our only hope of winning was to run other teams to death," says Daryl. "We'd pull games out during the fourth quarter if we pulled them out at all."

So Daryl was ordered to run. Sprints, stairs, and distance—up to 10 miles per day, every day, rain or shine.

"The coach wasn't going to check up on me, but he said he'd be able to tell if I'd put in the miles."

So all summer Daryl hit the pavement. Hard. It wasn't until a few weeks before school started that he could do 10 miles without wondering if he'd die.

The day Daryl reported to campus, the coach had his team lace up their running shoes for a 10-mile run.

"That's 10 miles *one way*," says Daryl. "Guys who performed to the coach's satisfaction got a return ride to campus.

"The others had a long hike home."

Daryl's coach knew something his team didn't: A 10-mile test was in their future. Unless they suffered a little all summer, they'd never pass the test.

Building grit slowly, a few sprints at a time, was worth it... but Daryl had to take that on faith. He believed that obeying the training schedule would pay off—and it did.

"On faith" is almost always necessary for grit-building obedience. You do it not because it necessarily feels good but because you trust Jesus knows something you don't know.

Because he wants you to be ready for what's coming your way.

FORGIVE THEM ANYWAY

It's hard enough to forgive friends who accidentally hurt you, friends who apologize when they realize what they've done.

But forgiving people who *purposely* hurt you or someone you love? And then don't care about what they've done?

That's hard. *That* takes spiritual grit.

It takes the sort of grit Jesus shows when, from the cross, he prays, "Father, forgive them, for they don't know what they are doing" (Luke 23:34).

Sorry to disagree, Jesus, but the religious leaders smirking in the distance and those soldiers rolling dice to see who wins your robe know *exactly* what they're doing: They're killing you.

Slowly.

Intentionally.

And they'll sleep just fine tonight.

What they don't understand is the significance of their actions. They don't know who they've nailed to that cross.

But even with the sound of their laugher ringing in your ears, you forgive them. And you ask God to do the same.*

That's the standard Jesus sets when it comes to forgiveness: Do it anyway...even if the people hammering spikes through your hands aren't the least bit sorry. Even if they think they're doing God a favor by murdering you.

That's the gritty kind of forgiveness Jesus expects from his disciples—then and now.

He makes it even more impossible by saying this: "If you forgive those who sin against you, your heavenly Father will forgive you. But if you refuse to forgive others, your Father will not forgive your sins" (Matthew 6:14-15).

Oh, great. Now flunking Forgiveness 101 means you don't get forgiven yourself.

This just gets better and better...

But here's the thing: While you can't muster up the grit to forgive on your own, with Jesus' help, it's possible.

In fact, it's *only* possible with Jesus' help.

On your own you can find a way to excuse bad behavior or repress the memory of what someone has done to you or a loved one. There's evil in the world, people are broken, abusers were abused—you know the drill.

But forgiveness—deep, lasting, soul-soothing forgiveness— that's the stuff of heaven. And that takes the help of someone who's been there.

Who, if anyone, needs your forgiveness—whether that person knows it or not?

And what, if anything, are you willing to do about it?

Read the entire account in Luke 23:26-38.

GRIT GROWER 19: SLOW FADE TO FORGIVENESS

Head to the dollar store and buy a helium balloon. Take a permanent marker with you, or pick one up while you're balloon shopping.

The balloon's design doesn't matter, but get one that's colorful and easy to see.

Take your balloon to an open field or parking lot—somewhere your view isn't blocked by trees or buildings.

Using the marker, write something you've found hard to forgive on the balloon. Be specific, but don't name names.

Invite Jesus to join you as you release the balloon. Ask him to stand beside you as the two of you watch it grow smaller, then smaller still, and then disappear altogether.

As you watch, ask Jesus this question: *How can you help the pain I feel fade away in the same way the balloon is fading into the distance?*

Listen carefully. The answer may require grit, but it will bring healing.

And Even Grittier

Write on your balloon, but don't release it.

Instead, carry it home, and tie it so it floats where others can see it. How does it feel to have the thing that's hard to forgive out in the open? In what ways do you feel more, or less, free because it's out in the open?

What did you discover about yourself as you talked with Jesus about forgiveness?

_____

_____

What did you discover about Jesus as the two of you watched the balloon disappear?

_____

_____

In what ways was this experience hard...and good?

_____

_____

Where was the spiritual grit in these experiences? What new strength have you noticed in yourself because of them?

_____

_____

GRIT GROWER 20: FORGIVING...YESTERDAY

Forgiving others isn't something to put off.

If you hang on to a hurt too long, it may become almost impossible to let it go. It becomes part of you, a piece of your story you let define you.

So do this: Think about yesterday.

In fact, pull out your calendar now or fire up your laptop to scheduling software that will walk you through the past 24 hours or so.

What happened yesterday that you could forgive now, rather than letting it simmer?

And in what way, if any, did you have a hand in those hard situations?

Maybe your words escalated a conflict rather than calmed it. Maybe your attitude sparked a fire or fanned the flames of an already heated moment.

Ask Jesus to help you remember and then do more than remember: forgive.

And Even Grittier

Have the conversation with Jesus as you're tackling that cleaning chore you've put off because you hate it.

Maybe your refrigerator would give the health department hives. Or you could plant corn in the carpet of your car and it would sprout. Or the dust bunnies under your bed are the size of dust buffaloes.

Ask Jesus to give you insight as you clean: How is leaving forgiveness for later like what happens when you leave cleaning for later?

What did you discover about yourself as you considered forgiving others and yourself?

_____

_____

How does deciding to forgive remind you of Jesus? of his friendship with you?

_____

_____

In what ways was this experience hard...and good?

_____

_____

Where was the spiritual grit in these experiences? Why, exactly, do we often put off doing hard things ?

_____

_____

GRIT GROWER 21: FORGIVENESS FLOWERS

Send a bouquet of flowers to someone you need to forgive. Something sunny and bright. Daisies, maybe.

Don't specify on the accompanying card why you're sending flowers; just sign the card and let that be enough.

Once you've tucked your credit card back in your wallet, reflect on this: How does it feel to invest in a failed or fractured relationship?

What will you say if the person on the receiving end of the bouquet gives you a call?

And Even Grittier

Same say-it-with-flowers activity.

Same investment made in a relationship that's on life support.

Probably best not to send flowers a second time to someone you need to forgive, but if you can't think of at least one other person who's hurt you, you're not trying.

This time, though, consider this: What will you say to Jesus—and yourself—if no call ever comes?

What did you discover about yourself as you sent flowers to someone who's wronged you?

How is what you've done for that person like what Jesus has done for you?

In what ways was this experience hard...and good?

Where was the spiritual grit in these experiences? How is what you did like what Jesus does with you every day?

SPIRITUAL GRIT MEETS...
FORGIVING INFIDELITY

Things weren't going well for Matt and his wife. Matt thought he understood the problem.

"I'm an auto parts sales rep, and I travel a lot," he says. "I figured once I got through the spring sales season I'd ratchet it back and be home more with Ashley and the kids. I thought that would get us reconnected."

But while Matt was out of town, sitting in a customer's waiting room, he got a text from Ashley asking him to call right away. It was an emergency, and Matt didn't recognize the number.

"It was her lawyer," says Matt. "She'd filed for divorce and had her lawyer notify me."

Matt canceled the remainder of his sales meetings and caught the first flight home. When he walked into the house, it was empty.

Ashley had packed up and gone, taking the kids with her.

And Matt had no idea where any of them were.

He phoned her parents and friends, but nobody knew or was willing to say where Ashley was living. It's as if his wife had vanished; not even her lawyer would offer anything more than a quick reassurance that she and the kids were safe.

A few days later Ashley's lawyer reached out to arrange a meeting in his office.

When Matt showed up, eager to find some way to reconcile with his wife, he found Ashley waiting with shocking news.

"She'd been having an affair," Matt says. "The affair was over, but she wanted out of our marriage. She wanted a chance to start fresh. She knew I'd never forgive her.

"And there was this: She was pregnant...with her lover's baby."

Matt stormed out of the office, slamming through doors until he found himself in the parking lot. He screamed. He pounded his fist against the trunk of his car.

How could he reconcile with a wife who'd been unfaithful, who was carrying a baby that wasn't his?

How could Matt ever forgive this?

"That's when I heard a voice," says Matt. "It said, 'But I forgave *you*.'"

Matt knew instantly whose voice he'd heard…and what was being asked of him. He felt his fury drain away, then made his way back upstairs to the lawyer's office.

"Ashley was stunned to see me," Matt says. She was equally amazed at what he told her: He was willing to give the marriage a try. Yes, it would be hard. Yes, there was plenty to work through and forgive on both sides—but he'd give it his all.

They're still together, Matt and Ashley.

When Ashley gave birth, an arranged adoption placed the baby with a family both Matt and Ashley knew. They quietly keep in touch and know the baby's loved and happy.

Matt's the first to admit he needed forgiveness, too. His workaholic tendencies don't excuse what Ashley did, but they help Matt understand why she was vulnerable and needy.

Matt's equally quick to say the industrial-strength forgiveness needed in his marriage took more than sheer willpower and determination.

"Jesus reached into our situation," he says. "Nobody else could have made this happen."

Spiritual grit? This situation is awash in it.

The grit of forgiveness. Of compassion. Of sacrifice.

It's all here…and it's no coincidence that Jesus is nearby.

As Matt said, "Nobody else could have made this happen."

EMBRACE TRANSFORMATION...
EVEN IF IT HURTS

Jesus' first disciples knew how to please God:

1) Learn the rules.
2) Obey the rules.
3) Repeat.

Toss in an occasional sacrificial lamb to smooth over the times rules were bent or broken, and everything's kosher.

It's the system Jesus' first disciples were taught in synagogue. It's what all the rabbis preached. As a system for making God happy, it's clear, clean, and predictable.

And then Jesus upsets everything, saying, "You have heard that our ancestors were told, 'You must not murder. If you commit murder, you are subject to judgment.'

"But I say, if you are even angry with someone, you are subject to judgment! If you call someone an idiot, you are in danger of being brought before the court. And if you curse someone, you are in danger of the fires of hell."*

That's when the disciples swallow hard and make a mental note: *We're gonna need a lot more sacrificial lambs.*

That God cares about more than their actions wasn't news—that message was hammered home throughout the psalms and the prophets. But because it's so much easier to look solely at actions, that's where many religious leaders in Jesus' day landed.

Not Jesus, though.

He's after more than mere compliance.

He wants to see transformation, and that goes far deeper than just doing. It's change from the inside out—and that both takes and builds spiritual grit.

It happens when we abide in Jesus, relying on him instead of ourselves, our circumstances, or others.

Jesus calls his followers to do more than just modify their outward behavior. He declares that, moving forward, their thoughts and motives are up for review, too.

And what was true for them is true for you, too.

So how does the notion that Jesus knows your thoughts and motivations strike you? Is being so well known by him a comfort... or something else?

Why?

Read the entire account in Matthew 5:21-26.

GRIT GROWER 22: MARK YOUR GROWTH

Remember when you were a child and your year-to-year growth was tracked by pencil marks on a doorjamb or pantry door?

You'd stand there in your bare feet, someone would lay a ruler on your head, and yet another line would appear that declared you were growing.

Growth as a disciple isn't measured in pencil marks. It's measured in transformation, in a changed heart and faithful living.

But that doesn't mean you can't pull out a ruler and pencil anyway.

Stand against a doorjamb and ask someone to indicate your height with a pencil mark. Then ask Jesus how you've been growing as a disciple. Compared to a year ago, where's transformation happening?

And Even Grittier

Invite someone who knows you well to be the one who makes the pencil mark; then risk asking: *How do you see transformation happening in my life? In what ways am I different from the person I was a year or two ago?*

That's a tough question, so give your friend time to consider his or her answer.

It's tough because the transformation may be internal and gradual, not yet visible from the outside.

It's tough because perhaps the transformation is subtle, something only you've noticed.

And it's tough because your friend might honestly not see any transformation in you—just your circumstances. And that's a hard message to deliver.

So ask, wait, and see what Jesus does with the conversation.

What did you discover about yourself as you talked with your friend about transformation?

_____

_____

In what ways are you being transformed by your relationship with Jesus?

_____

_____

In what ways was this experience hard...and good?

_____

_____

Where was the spiritual grit in these experiences? What is usually true about all of your transforming experiences?

_____

_____

It's tough to be transformed until you're ready to change.

And it's tough to change until you admit that, just maybe, you don't know everything and you don't have it all together. And *that* is a grit-growing admission.

See where this is headed?

Do this: Try something and fail. Fail big. Fail in a way that leaves no doubt that you're failing. Here's how...

Get a half-dozen small balls, empty plastic soda bottles, or hacky sacks, and in the privacy of your home, try juggling.

If you're like most non-jugglers, this won't go well. Prepare to be humbled.

The truth is, while juggling doesn't look all that hard, to be transformed into a capable juggler, you need help. Coaching. Someone to show you the ropes.

Until then you're probably just one more person chasing rubber balls around the room.

And Even Grittier

Gather up your juggling supplies, and find a spot where people can see you. A subway or bus stop. Outside the door of a grocery store. Anywhere you're out of the way but still in the spotlight.

And fail there.

If someone who actually knows how to juggle has mercy on you and offers a quick tutorial, humbly accept the help.

Transformation often travels hand in hand with humility. So be humble.

And if you already know how to juggle, pick another activity. Singing opera comes to mind.

What did you discover about yourself and humility? Would people who know you well say you're a humble person? Why or why not?

_____

_____

How did Jesus model humility? What has that meant to you?

_____

_____

In what ways was this experience hard...and good?

_____

_____

Where was the spiritual grit in these experiences? Why is it hard sometimes for you to be humble? Why is it easy?

_____

_____

GRIT GROWER 24: MAKE SPACE

Jesus didn't settle for wedging himself into the regular routines of his first disciples.

He insisted they clear their calendars and be with him around the clock, soaking up what he said, how he lived, what he valued.

He wanted focused attention, something we current disciples are very, very bad at giving him.

Until now.

Because now—or as soon as you can arrange it—you'll unplug for 24 hours.

That means no video games, television, or media of any kind that's not absolutely required for you to stay employed.

Instead, use that time to make space for transformation. For thinking about Jesus. For listening for his voice.

For just one day, don't expect him to shout over your distractions. Focus on him instead.

Invite transformation.

And Even Grittier

Add fasting to your 24 hours of focused attention on Jesus.

This spiritual discipline is more than simply not eating. It's setting aside food so you can sharpen your focus on Jesus.

Take the usual precautions—drink lots of water and be sure medications that are to be taken with food can safely be consumed.

Then commit to a prayerful, focused, media-free, 24-hour fast as you make space for Jesus to nudge your transformation forward.

•···•

What happened during your 24 hours of focused attention on Jesus?

_____

_____

What did you discover about Jesus? about yourself?

_____

_____

In what ways was this experience hard...and good?

_____

_____

Where was the spiritual grit in these experiences? At some point your perseverance was tested. How did that affect your relationship with Jesus?

_____

_____

SPIRITUAL GRIT MEETS...
THE MALL

Seasonal temp at the mall. Ten bucks an hour. No benefits. Nonstop, canned, insanely annoying Christmas music.

Sarah doesn't really want this job. But with two kids and bills stacking up, she's doing what she needs to do.

So here she is, stocking shelves, cashiering, serving customers, and watching for shoplifters.

Oh, and Sarah has one more daily duty: swallowing her pride.

"Five months ago, before a corporate restructuring, I was a VP in an accounting office," Sarah says. "Nice office, flexible hours, someone keeping my coffee cup full."

She's confident she'll find another management job, but she's unsure when that will happen. So for now she's endlessly refolding the same sweaters and running credit card after credit card through the scanner.

"When people who know me come into the store, they don't know what to say. Some offer me their sympathy. Others turn around and leave. Some look right through me," says Sarah.

"Don't get me wrong: There's nothing wrong with being a clerk," Sarah says. "It's an honorable job. And at this point I'd mop floors for a paycheck."

Sarah laughs. "Actually, I *do* mop floors for a paycheck. I clean the employee bathroom, too."

Sarah vows that when she lands in the corner office again, she won't take for granted the people who work for her.

And she's gotten past defining herself by her job title.

"I was measuring my worth by what I did and how many people I supervised," Sarah says. "This temp job has helped me see myself—and others—differently."

Sarah is earning more than a paycheck at the mall. She's also earning grit—being humbled does that for you.

And as Sarah leans into the learning, she's building spiritual grit, too.

She's being transformed from the inside out.

JUDGE CAREFULLY

It's exactly the sort of thing that raises the disciples' blood pressure—and it happens all the time.

It seems every time they turn around someone's interrupting Jesus. Demanding his attention. Derailing him as he's on his way to somewhere important.

This time it's a woman who shows up at a dinner party.

Nobody notices her as she comes in—Simon of Bethany is hosting Jesus and the disciples in his home, and they're busy talking and eating. But she makes her way over to Jesus and empties an alabaster jar of expensive perfume over his head.

A nice gesture but not one every disciple appreciates.

They throw up their hands in exasperation. Why didn't the woman donate the perfume instead? It's expensive—*astoundingly* expensive—and could have been sold to provide money for the poor.

Why, it's just this kind of short-sighted theatrics that...

Jesus rises to the blushing woman's defense, quieting his complaining disciples with a command and a question. "Leave her alone," he says. "Why criticize her for doing such a good thing to me? You will always have the poor among you, and you can help them whenever you want to. But you will not always have me" (Mark 14:6-7).

The disciples have misjudged both the woman and Jesus.

She wasn't being wasteful; she was worshipping.

And Jesus wasn't counting costs; he was counting down the days until his body would be anointed again, this time for burial.

The disciples have forgotten what Jesus said earlier about judging others:

"Do not judge others, and you will not be judged. For you will be treated as you treat others. The standard you use in judging is the standard by which you will be judged" (Matthew 7:1-2).

Jesus isn't suggesting that you and the rest of his followers never judge situations or people. He's simply saying that the standards you use to pass judgment may well be applied to you.

Which is about the most powerful motivation to develop restraint that Jesus could possibly trot out for his followers.*

If you're quick to judge, expect the same. If you always assume negative motives behind others' actions, that's a standard you might see applied to yourself.

How do you feel, knowing that Jesus reserves the right to judge you using the same standards you use to judge others?

Happy thought...or something else?

*Read the entire account in Mark 14:1-9.

GRIT GROWER 25: PEOPLE WATCHING

Find a spot that's good for people watching.

A public park. The zoo. A bench at the mall.

Then do this: Decide which people you're drawn to and which you aren't. Two lists—people you'd welcome if they were to sit down next to you and those who, as far as you're concerned, can keep on walking.

Mentally sort passersby for five or ten minutes.

Then ask yourself: *How did I decide who's in each group? How did I pass judgment?*

Jot your thoughts in the margins of this page. You won't be describing how you think you *should* judge others; you'll describe how you *actually* judge others.

And no matter how uncomfortable the thought, you do judge others. We all do.

Review what you wrote. What sort of picture do your comments paint? Is it a portrait of a person who's caring?

curious? open—or closed?

And how comfortable are you with others judging you in the same way you've judged them? Explain.

And Even Grittier

Being called judgmental is one of the ultimate insults of our time.

But risk it: Invite another Jesus-follower to join you at the mall.

Do the people-watching described earlier, but quietly compare notes—about who ends up on your lists and why.

Then, together, read Matthew 7:1-2 and grapple with Jesus' words. If he's serious, what does that mean about how the two of you live your daily lives? What, if anything, do you want to change? What would it take to make those changes?

"Do not judge others, and you will not be judged. For you will be treated as you treat others. The standard you use in judging is the standard by which you will be judged" (Matthew 7:1-2).

What did you discover about yourself through these judging experiences?

_____

_____

What did you discover about Jesus?

_____

_____

In what ways was this experience hard...and good?

_____

_____

Where was the spiritual grit in these experiences? What are the pros and cons of self-knowledge?

_____

_____

GRIT GROWER 26: WELL, YOUR HONOR...

Find a reality television show filmed in a small-claims court. Google can help; search for Judge Wapner, Judge Judy, or Judge Mathis.

Small-claims court is where people who have disputes can argue their case without lawyers. A judge listens to both sides and quickly announces what he or she thinks is a fair resolution.

Watch a few cases—they go fast—and decide if you agree with the judge's rulings.

What would you do if *you* were the one wearing the black robe?

And is passing judgment in a courtroom something you can see yourself doing? What's your level of confidence you'd be good at judging when the cameras are rolling?

An even better question: What's your level of confidence that the judgments you make now—about people, situations, and yourself—are good decisions?

And Even Grittier

Field trip!

Ask another Jesus-follower to join you in your community's small-claims court.

Watch a few cases; then grab a cup of coffee with your friend.

Talk about how Jesus wants to transform you when it comes to being judgmental. Is he wanting you not to make judgments at all, make better judgments, or something else?

Roll around in that mud puddle awhile, and then make a judgment about who's going to pick up the check.

As you thought about judging others, what did you discover about yourself?

_____

_____

What did you discover about Jesus?

_____

_____

In what ways was this experience hard...and good?

_____

_____

Where was the spiritual grit in these experiences? Jesus said we'd be judged by the same standard we judge others. What do you like and not like about that?

_____

_____

GRIT GROWER 27: A QUESTION FOR YOU, OFFICER...

You know a police officer, right?

No? Ask around—someone you know does. Get a name and an introduction.

Police officers make judgment calls all day long.

Who's a threat and who isn't.

Who's dangerous and who's just distracted or angry.

Who to pull over, who to ticket, and who to let off with a warning.

Police officers' ability to make quick judgments can save lives—theirs and yours.

Do this: Ask an officer how he or she makes decisions. What factors play into deciding if there's a problem. What signals cause that officer to move closer for a better look.

See what you can learn—good and bad—about judging others.

And Even Grittier

Call your local police station and ask if you (or you and a Jesus-following friend) can ride along in a patrol car.

Some departments allow this; some don't. You won't know unless you ask.

While in the squad car, observe how the officer makes decisions. Ask what that officer has learned over the years that's sharpened an ability to make quick, on-target judgments.

Be respectful...and pay attention. You're seeing experience in action.

You might even be seeing spiritual grit.

•···•

What did you discover about yourself during these experiences?

_____

_____

What did you discover about passing judgment?

_____

_____

In what ways was this experience hard...and good?

_____

_____

Where was the spiritual grit in these experiences? Why is it so easy to judge others harshly and so hard to judge them fairly?

_____

_____

SPIRITUAL GRIT MEETS...
MISJUDGING THE MOMENT

It was Mike's first-ever shift as a bell-ringer next to a Salvation Army kettle, and he feared it might be his last.

"I was outside a Safeway store and doing everything I was supposed to do," Mike says. "I was ringing the bell, wishing people 'Merry Christmas,' even handing out little candy canes I brought with me."

And that's when a low-rider muscle car screeched up next to the curb and slammed on its brakes.

Mike heard the car coming before he saw it.

"There were huge bass speakers on the back deck, and the whole car vibrated. I'm not sure what song was playing, but it was insanely loud and equally obscene."

The guy who leapt out of the car came straight for Mike, who was sure he was about to become the first bell-ringer in history to have his kettle boosted in broad daylight.

"The guy was scowling," Mike says. "He had tattoos everywhere and wore a scuffed leather jacket that looked like it had been through a few fights. I remember thinking, 'I've got to pay attention to what this guy looks like so I can describe him to the police.'"

As the man approached Mike, he reached behind his back and under his jacket. Mike nearly turned and ran. "I just knew he was reaching for a gun," Mike says.

But what came out from under the jacket was no gun.

It was a wallet.

"He reached in and pulled out a $20 bill. Then he stuffed it in the bucket, gave me a nod, and jogged back to the car.

"He was gone before I could lift my jaw off the pavement."

It took a moment, but then Mike felt it burning: shame.

"I was completely wrong about this guy," Mike admits. "He went out of his way to be charitable. He gave more than anyone else. But I judged him and decided he was a robber—all because of my own bias and fear.

"That was a valuable lesson for me," Mike says. "It's changed how I look at people and how quickly I judge them."

And there's the grit: Jesus used what Mike experienced to transform him.

It's easy to make snap judgments—natural and even useful at times. But pausing before passing judgment?

That's hard.

That takes grit.

BE ALL-IN

Jesus and his 12 closest followers are together, celebrating the Passover meal in a cozy, lamp-lit room. Jesus has been distracted all evening; there's clearly something weighing heavily on his mind.

And then Jesus says this: "I am the way, the truth, and the life. No one can come to the Father except through me" (John 14:6).

The disciples trade nervous glances because that kind of talk can get you in trouble. *Serious* trouble.

The disciples have heard Jesus say things like this before, but not while they were sitting in Jerusalem. Not where a curious ear at the door might catch Jesus' declaration and carry it straight across town to a high priest looking for any excuse to charge Jesus with blasphemy.

Or worse, that same someone might tell the Romans.

Romans ruled a vast empire, so they'd adopted a live-and-let-live approach to religion. You could believe in whatever local gods you wanted, as long as you also acknowledged *their* gods.

Which is exactly what Jesus isn't doing.

He's declaring that he's *it*. Forget Jupiter and Juno; Jesus is tossing Roman deities out like so many rotten figs.

Jesus is saying to believe in him—and *only* him. There's no room for splitting your allegiance or hedging your bets. Either you're all-in with him, or you're looking in the wrong place.

Which is a very, very dangerous thing to say.

If Jesus is serious—and the disciples can see he is—he's announcing yet again that they have a choice: They can be all-in with him...or not. There's no middle ground.

What they *can't* do is be lukewarm about him, and neither can anyone else.

So in that shadowed room, two unspoken questions hang in the air:

Do the disciples believe Jesus is who he says he is...or not?

And what are they willing to do about it?*

Those same two questions wait for anyone—like you—who's following Jesus. They slice the cloth right down the middle, and you're on one side or the other.

If you believe in Jesus, that's fine, but it's nothing special. Lots of people believe in Jesus. It's easy to do that. Comforting and inspirational, even.

But believing that Jesus is who he says he is? that he's *the* way, *the* truth, and *the* life, and nobody comes to the Father except through him?

That's the harder question.

So for you, the same two questions that floated through the minds of 12 people seated around a low table with Jesus:

Do I believe Jesus is who he says he is...or not?

And what am I willing to do about it?

Answer carefully. There's a wealth of grit to be mined in those decisions.

*Read the entire account in John 14:6-14.

GRIT GROWER 28: TUB TIME

It's time to be all-in...your bathtub.

So do this: Fill your tub with warm water. Place a fluffy towel nearby. Add bubbles, and light a candle if you're so inclined. Play some relaxing music.

Do your level best to transform your bathroom into a five-star spa.

Then slip out of your bathrobe and slide into the warm, inviting water—without disturbing it. Without making a splash or prompting a ripple.

If possible without even raising the water level.

Try as you might, you can't do it. When you're all-in a bathtub, it shows.

It's the same with Jesus. If you're all-in, it shows in what you say, how you live, how you describe him to others.

As you soak, talk with Jesus about how you're doing with being all-in. Does he see you that way? If not, what does he want you to do about it?

And Even Grittier

Still in the tub?

Good—stay there.

Stay there as the warm water grows tepid, then cool, then uncomfortably cold.

Don't move as you think about this: How willing are you to stay all-in with Jesus when things get hard?

Pray for grit—because challenging, chilly times are coming.

Oh, and climb on out of there and towel off. You'll catch your death of cold.

•···•

Other than how much you needed a relaxing bath, what did you discover about yourself through these experiences?

_____

_____

What did you hear from Jesus? What, if anything, did he say to you?

_____

_____

In what ways was this experience hard...and good?

_____

_____

Where was the spiritual grit in these experiences? How does an all-in attitude affect your ability to persevere?

_____

_____

GRIT GROWER 29: FIFTY AND COUNTING

A friendship with Jesus is a lot like marriage.

Both relationships are marked by commitment. Passion. An expectation the relationship will go the distance.

Do this: Find a couple who's been married at least 50 years and ask if you can talk with them about why, in a world where so many marriages fail, theirs has lasted.

Here are some questions you might ask:

- What do you do as a couple that protects your marriage?
- Would you say you're all-in your marriage? What does that look like?
- What's helped you weather the hard times in your marriage?
- What advice would you give younger couples who want their marriages to thrive?

Take notes—this is grit served up on a platter.

And remember to send a thank-you card.

And Even Grittier

Maybe the idea of being passionately committed to Jesus feels...awkward.

Committed, yes. But passionate?

That's just creepy.

Except if you're *not* passionate, if you don't take your commitment to Jesus at least as seriously as you take wedding vows, you won't stick with him. You'll wander away and not come back.

Do this: Invite a few Jesus-followers to join you for a public commitment to Jesus. Even if you've been confirmed, dedicated, and baptized, read the following aloud, in public, where witnesses see and hear you. It's a reminder to you and a statement to the world: When it comes to Jesus, you're all-in.

"Jesus, I, [your name], promise to love, honor, and obey you. I will abide in you in sickness and in health, for richer or for poorer, as long as I live. I forsake all others and trust in you alone as my Savior and Lord."

You may now cut the cake and serve it to your witnesses.

•···•

What did you discover about being all-in and committed from these experiences?

_____

_____

What did you learn about yourself?

_____

_____

In what ways was this experience hard...and good?

_____

_____

Where was the spiritual grit in these experiences? When has it cost you to follow Jesus, and why did you pay that price?

_____

_____

GRIT GROWER 30: REMINDERS

Ask a friend to text you a half-dozen times tomorrow, always with the same message: "What's all-in look like right now?"

If a text arrives while you're at work, pause to consider how to answer the question. Whether you're meeting with people, making a decision, or pushing ahead on a project, how does it look to do that while being all-in with Jesus?

Ditto if a text arrives while you're at home.

Or with friends.

Or at the gym, browsing online, or driving to the hardware store.

All-in. What's that look like for you?

And Even Grittier

Wrap a bandage around one of your fingers.

Whenever you see it, let it be a reminder that Jesus wraps your life with love and care.

It's a reminder to you to be intentional about following Jesus in every situation, every conversation, every encounter throughout your day.

Here's what makes this gritty: When anyone asks you about the bandage, explain why you're wearing it and who you are in Jesus.

You're a disciple.

You're all-in.

What did you discover about being all-in with Jesus through these experiences?

_____

_____

In what ways was this experience hard...and good?

_____

_____

Where was the spiritual grit in these experiences? What typically motivates you to go all-in with something or someone, and why?

_____

_____

GRIT GROWER 31: PRIORITIES

Your life can get busy. Probably *does* get busy, as you're pushed and pulled in different directions by people and projects you could or should get done.

So you set priorities. Well, you set them or discover that other people are setting them for you as you react to what others want you to do.

Today you'll pick a third option. You'll invite Jesus to set your priorities for you.

But go into this with your eyes open: Asking Jesus to take charge is a guaranteed jump into grit territory. He may take you to unexpected places, steer you in a new direction.

Do it anyway.

Ask Jesus to set your priorities and agenda for the next 24 hours—your tasks, social calendar, entertainment, the whole enchilada.

Ask...then listen.
Listen...and then do.
That's being all-in.

And Even Grittier

Put your wallet or purse on the table, too.
Invite Jesus to speak into how you spend your money as well as how you spend your time during the next 24 hours.

What did you discover about yourself when you allowed Jesus to tell you how to use your time and resources for a day?

What did you discover about Jesus and what he values?

In what ways was this experience hard...and good?

Where was the spiritual grit in these experiences? What did you discover about Jesus as you moved through them?

SPIRITUAL GRIT MEETS...
THE WALL

While on staff at a northern California ranch for troubled kids, Nick got an assignment from the ranch director: Build a wall.

"It was a retaining wall," Nick remembers.

The wall wasn't anything big—maybe 10 feet long and 2 feet high.

Move some dirt, level the ground, throw up a concrete wall.

Except Nick had a problem: He had no idea how to build a wall—and said so.

"Figure it out," the director said.

And then there was this: Northern California was experiencing the worst concrete shortage since...forever.

Nick didn't know you could *have* a concrete shortage but quickly found out otherwise. Large suppliers wouldn't return his calls. Smaller suppliers were sold out. Even big-box stores had back-ordered bags of concrete mix.

There wasn't a speck of concrete available anywhere.

When the director demanded to know why he wasn't seeing progress on the wall, Nick explained it wasn't his fault. What could he do?

"He told me to go to the suppliers' warehouses, pound on doors, and beg. To go sweep their loading docks until I had enough mix. Or to find a way to build the wall without concrete.

"I had one week to build that wall, or I'd be fired," Nick says.

So Nick asked around. Was there a way to build a retaining wall without using concrete? Could he find enough rock? recruit enough help to muscle their way through the project in time?

There was, he could, and they did.

The wall was up on time.

It took Nick a few years, but it finally dawned on him that his boss's unreasonable demand wasn't about the wall at all.

"It was about me," Nick says. "I was always talking my way out of hard work, and this was his way of building something in me. I couldn't weasel my way out of the job—and I couldn't make excuses."

Nick's had some wins in life, but that wall is toward the top of his list.

"People know me as someone who keeps his word and follows through," he says. "That all started with the wall. I was given something hard to do and then forced to rise to the occasion."

When his son was struggling, Nick took him on a road trip halfway across the country so they could sit on the wall—which was still standing, 30 years later—and talk about doing hard things.

That talk changed his son's life…just as building the wall changed Nick's.

It's where he grew grit. Where he learned to ask for and accept help.

Where he learned that, with God's help, he could do the impossible.

SPIRITUAL GRIT MEETS...
ALCOHOLICS ANONYMOUS

Two times a week. That's how often you'll find Ron at an Alcoholics Anonymous meeting.

Rain or shine, under clear skies or in a blizzard, he's firing up his Honda Civic and making his way to a circle of folding chairs in a church basement.

Twice a week, no matter what.

No missing. No excuses. Not once.

Not for Ron.

"I remember what life was like before I got sober," he says. "I know that if I go back to that life I'll die." So it's been twice a week for Ron, week after week, month after month.

For 32 years.

Ron's all-in because he knows the cost of being anything less.

He also happens to be a Christian and was a pastor until alcoholism swept his family and pulpit away. And when asked why many AA members seem more committed to their cause than Christians seem committed to Jesus, Ron doesn't have to think long before answering.

"It's because a lot of us with addictions see this as a matter of life or death," he says. "If I start drinking again, I know I'll die. If the guy sitting across the table from me takes crystal meth again, he'll die, and he knows it.

"But most people who follow Jesus aren't all that serious about it. They're doing fine whether they remember to pray or not, whether they go to church or not. They don't see their faith as a matter of life or death."

Ron pauses a moment and shifts in his chair.

Then he quietly says this: "They're wrong, but they don't know that yet."

Do you hear the grit in Ron's reply?

His is a voice of experience, of someone who's fallen and fallen hard, only to be pulled back to his feet by Jesus and people acting in Jesus' name. He's a different man than he once was, and that's one way to tell grit has found a home.

Jesus has transformed Ron, and now, through Ron, he's transforming others.

GET USED TO UNCOMFORTABLE

Jesus' dozen disciples are excited.

They've watched Jesus heal lepers and cast out demons, but always from the sidelines. Now he's pulled them together for a chat as he's sending them out to see if they can do what they've seen him do.

This is big stuff. This is where they make Jesus proud.

Jesus has outlined the mission. Covered the logistics. Communicated the importance of what they'll be doing and why they're doing it.

And now there's nervous energy crackling around the room as Jesus waits for his followers to quiet down. Then, as they hang on to every word, he says this:

"You will be handed over to the courts and will be flogged with whips in the synagogues. You will stand trial before governors and kings because you are my followers...all nations will hate you because you are my followers...Don't be afraid of those who want to kill your body" (Matthew 10:17-18, 22, 28).

As pep talks go, that's something of a letdown.*

But it's Jesus' honest take on what's coming. If you're following him, you'd best grow some grit because—like it or not—things will get hard.

As in hate-you, hurt-you, drag-you-into-court hard.

Jesus doesn't sugarcoat the cost of following him. If you pursue the kingdom of God with anything approaching passion, you'll collide with the culture around you.

Your values won't align with many of the people in your life.

You'll march to the beat of a drummer some people can't—or won't—hear.

You'll encounter conflict, and there's no guarantee Jesus will do anything to sand those rough edges off your life. In fact, he may choose to do just the *opposite*. He may leave them there, snagging you at every turn.

"Uncomfortable" may well become your new normal.

Does Jesus care that you're experiencing discomfort? Sure. If you're like most people, you measure his friendship in part by whether he does something to cause hard stuff to stop.

That's what friends do, right? They remember your birthdays without noticing you're getting older. They make sympathetic noises when you're sad.

And when it's moving day, they show up with work gloves and a pickup truck.

Friends are supposed to be people who make our lives easier. People who see us wince and offer a back rub.

So why does Jesus claim to be your friend and then announce that hanging around with him will usher no end of hard stuff into your life? Hard stuff that he apparently has no intention of shielding you from?

From his perspective, the hard you encounter is often good. It drives you to him, causes you to rely on him. It's fertile soil for growing spiritual grit.

Yes, there's rough water ahead—you can count on it. But take heart in knowing this: You're not navigating it alone.

Your friend Jesus is with you.

If it's true that following Jesus puts you in a place where you experience conflict with your culture—what's it say if you're *not* experiencing conflict? if your journey is smooth and seamless?

When's the last time your allegiance to Jesus caused you to bump up against conflict? And what might it mean if that's not happening?

Read the entire account in Matthew 10:5-42.

When things get uncomfortable, it's easy to read that as a signal it's time to move along, to find a path with fewer obstacles in your way.

But remember: When you follow Jesus, "hard" is often just another way to say "good."

So find something you stopped doing because it was hard, and finish it.

The project gathering dust on your workbench that was more complicated than you expected.

The novel you wrote until page 97 and then let die a slow death.

The diet you abandoned when you realized chocolate wasn't allowed.

The friendship you let die of neglect because it required forgiveness.

Go finish something hard. Something that takes grit to bring in for a landing.

And Even Grittier

Finishing something builds grit.

Finishing something for someone else, something that takes considerable effort, drops a shovel full of grit into your life.

What's something that someone in your life can't do?

Pulling leaves out of a gutter, moving a refrigerator so the floor can get a good cleaning—anything that puts you at the intersection of Listening to Jesus and Uncomfortable.

That's where you're headed.

So go volunteer.

Let Jesus build some grit in your life.

• •

What are you discovering about yourself as you struggle with finishing something—for yourself or someone else?

_____

_____

What are you discovering about Jesus?

_____

_____

In what ways was this experience hard...and good?

_____

_____

Where was the spiritual grit in these experiences? What's different about people who quit halfway through challenges compared to those who don't?

_____

_____

GRIT GROWER 33: HUGS

Make a large sign that says, "Free hugs."

Go stand in a busy spot.

See who takes you up on your offer.

Going out on a limb here, but we're guessing it will be uncomfortable...for lots of reasons.

But that's not necessarily a bad thing, right?

Not if you invite Jesus along.

And Even Grittier

Up the ante.

Turn your sign over and write, "Free hugs and affirmations."

You've now committed yourself to share not only hugs but also kind words with people you've never met.

You'll be handing out sincere compliments. Positive observations. Upbeat inspiration.

Perhaps even insights shared with you courtesy of the Holy Spirit.

Every encounter is an adventure, one in which you lean on Jesus.

And that's the very definition of growing grit.

What did these experiences teach you about yourself?

_____

_____

What did you discover about Jesus?

_____

_____

In what ways was this experience hard...and good?

_____

_____

Where was the spiritual grit in these experiences? Which is easier: to affirm others through your words or actions? Why?

_____

_____

GRIT GROWER 34: PREPARE TO BE FLOORED

You've gone to great lengths to make your bed comfortable.

You've picked the right mattress. Found the perfect pillow. Added clean sheets and a soft, warm blanket or two.

Well, for at least one night, forget them all.

For one night you're sleeping on the floor.

Will you be uncomfortable? Probably—but that's one entrance ramp to grit.

Will it be hard to sleep? Maybe—but you'll be awake so you can pray. Also a way to build grit.

Will you really do this? We hope so—because sometimes Hard = Good, and the only way to see if this is one of those times is to grab a pillow, blanket, and positive attitude and stretch out on the floor for a night.

Happy dreams.

And Even Grittier

Same activity—but outside.

If you have a weather-appropriate tent or can borrow one, you're in great shape. If your car has reclining seats and the temperature won't dip below 40 degrees, you're ahead of the game, too.

However you do it—in a tent, a tepee, or a lean-to—sleep outside tonight. Alone or with someone else; that doesn't matter.

Just remember to invite Jesus along.

And, as you twist and turn, trying to get comfortable on that patio recliner, ask him this: *What can you teach me through this? How much does my desire for comfort get in the way of doing what you want me to do?*

•···•

What did these experiences teach you about yourself and your desire for comfort?

_____

_____

What did you discover about Jesus?

_____

_____

In what ways was this experience hard...and good?

_____

_____

Where was the spiritual grit in these experiences?

_____

_____

SPIRITUAL GRIT MEETS...
A CABIN

Good luck getting in touch with Shawn Gabriel.

You might catch him when he's in town, but that doesn't happen often.

Usually he's out at his place, the one he built on his sister-in-law's property about a dozen miles west of the county line. It's a cabin—a fairly nice one, actually—and he and Angie have lived there the past 10 years.

There's no electricity, and the water comes from a well, but it's a comfortable place anyway.

Oh—and there's next to no cellphone reception, so you won't be calling him.

Still, a comfortable place.

A lot of snow in the winter on a quarter-mile of gravel driveway, so there's that to clear every few weeks until spring. Rattlers have the run of the fields all summer. And nobody's interested in delivering a pizza—Shawn's checked.

But, all in all, a comfortable place—at least compared to where they used to live.

Shawn worked for one of the big-box retailers all through his 20s and 30s, and just before he hit 40, he landed the corporate job he'd wanted all along. His pay almost doubled, but so did the hours, and he'd been putting in plenty already.

Nights. Weekends. Holidays. Shawn spent them visiting stores or meeting with managers. When he wasn't with colleagues, he was nose down in spreadsheets searching for a way to squeeze out one more point of profitability.

Angie and the kids seldom saw him and eventually got used to it. They hardly missed him; he was just someone who floated through occasionally, usually too exhausted to do much but drift off to sleep in front of a game on TV.

Shawn had convinced himself he was doing it all for his family. He'd dig in for the duration, earn a pile of money, pay off the McMansion, and then have every day from his 55th birthday on to enjoy family and friends.

Besides, what did Angie have to complain about? She lived in the nicest house on a block of great houses. All the latest conveniences. Everything she wanted was right at her fingertips.

But Shawn's plan went off the rails with the arrival of a heart attack when he was all of 52.

Shawn nearly died. *Did* die but was rushed to the hospital and revived.

And when he was wrapping up therapy, Angie dropped a question in his lap: Did he want to live or die? Did he want to be with her and the kids or not?

If he decided to stick around, life was going to get uncomfortable, financially and otherwise. It was going to get gritty.

Shawn chose to live, which meant his job had to go.

He still works, but in a shop out back of the cabin. He walks the 20 feet to his kitchen to have lunch with Angie every day and wraps up in the shop by 6:00 each night.

The kids are grown but come by most weekends, and they're happy to spend time with him. He's now the dad they never had, the dad they always wanted.

So good luck getting in touch with Shawn Gabriel.

He's busy living the most rewarding, comforting, uncomfortable life he could have imagined.

SPIRITUAL GRIT MEETS... NEIL ARMSTRONG

Larry taught at the University of Cincinnati decades ago but remembers one particular lunch at the University Club as if it happened yesterday.

"I have no idea what I ate," Larry says, "But getting seated? *That* I'll never forget."

Larry was waiting with two colleagues, Bruce and Dave, as the hostess escorted a couple in front of them to a table. And Dave was complaining—loudly—about a recent flight.

"He usually flew first class but had been bounced to a middle seat back in coach," Larry says. "The flight was late taking off and, given his discomfort, seemed to last forever.

"Dave was fired up, ready to lead an armed insurrection against the airline. Nobody in the lobby could avoid hearing him."

That included a guy standing behind Dave who listened in, nodding politely as Dave cursed the airline for its inhumane treatment of passengers—especially how they squeezed bottoms into tiny seats with no leg room.

During Dave's rant the hostess returned, and Larry saw her eyes widen. She brushed past Larry's little group to pull the man behind them into the restaurant.

"Dave came *unglued*," says Larry. "When she circled back, the hostess got an earful about ignoring three hardworking instructors to seat some yahoo who showed up after we did."

The hostess asked if Dave knew who the man was.

Dave didn't know and didn't care. His time was valuable. Did she have any idea who *he* was?

"That's when she told us she'd just seated Neil Armstrong—the first man on the moon. He was teaching at the university, too, and the university president and deans were waiting for him in the conference room."

A long silence followed. A long, shuffling silence as Dave tried to think of something—*anything*—to say.

Finally, Bruce spoke.

"So, to sum up, Dave: You just complained about how uncomfortable you were on a flight from Dallas. Limited leg room. Uncomfortable seat. Uncomfortable 20-minute delay.

"You complained to a guy who crawled into a capsule the size of a washing machine—along with two other guys. And they flew to the *moon* and back.

"Just wondering: What do you think Neil Armstrong's got that you don't have?"

Larry says Dave asked if they could all forget the incident ever happened.

"But as it's been almost 40 years and I still bring it up whenever I see him," Larry says, "I doubt *that's* going to happen."

LEAN INTO HARD CONVERSATIONS

Peter's worried about Jesus.

Lately, Jesus has talked about going to Jerusalem, dying, and rising from the dead. It's depressing, and furthermore, it's scaring away the crowds.

Whatever happened to water-into-wine Jesus? The Jesus who scooped up kids and gave James and John a hard time about their tempers? That's the Jesus Peter loves following.

But this new Jesus? The one spending more and more time alone in the hills, praying?

That guy's scaring Peter.

So Peter takes Jesus aside for a little man-to-man chat.

Peter assures Jesus there's no need for worry because none of Jesus' predictions will come true. No Jerusalem, no dying, no coming back from the tomb. If Jesus sticks with Peter, it'll all be fine.

That's when Jesus snaps back with something sharp and unfiltered.

"Get away from me, Satan! You are a dangerous trap to me. You are seeing things merely from a human point of view, not from God's" (Matthew 16:23).

If that sounds harsh, there's a reason: It is. Here's Peter trying to help, and he gets his head handed to him. What has he done that's so wrong?

Peter doesn't see that Jesus has no choice but to face the cross if he's to reconcile God and mankind. Jesus is going to Jerusalem because it's part of God's plan.

And along comes Peter suggesting Jesus abandon that plan, something Satan would love for Jesus to do. At the moment, Peter and Satan are on the same page.

Peter's heart may be in the right place, but that doesn't change the fact that he's completely, dangerously misreading the situation.

So Jesus sets him straight.

It takes spiritual grit to journey with Jesus. And it takes a special measure of that grit to stay when Jesus has called you a devil to your face.

Peter is at a crossroads. He can get offended and leave, as many before him have, or choose to keep following Jesus.

He chooses Jesus...and turns his face toward Jerusalem.

Peter's a lot like you—and the rest of us who tag along after Jesus.

He's a work in progress.

More than once Peter requires a midcourse correction to keep him on track, and some of those come in the form of pointed conversations. Peter isn't alone; all the disciples are occasionally on the receiving end of tough-love conversations with Jesus.

But even as Jesus puts Peter in his place, Peter feels it: love. Jesus loves him enough to pause and deal with him. To correct, confront, encourage.

Jesus is building spiritual grit in Peter, and as hard as that can be at times, Peter loves Jesus for it.*

How about you? How do you respond when Jesus has hard conversations with you? Do you see that as love...or something else?

*Read the entire account in Matthew 16:13-28.

You'll need two pieces of paper, a pen, and a match. Ready?

Do this: On one sheet of paper, write five things about yourself that are true. Undeniably true—you know them to be fact because you've had them confirmed time and again.

Maybe it's that you've got a great sense of humor. Or that you're a gifted pianist. Or a solid friend.

Five things. Put them in writing.

On the other sheet of paper, write five things about yourself that aren't true—but you find yourself believing sometimes.

That at heart you're a failure. That you're not enough. That if people really knew you they'd walk away from you.

Put those in writing, too.

Now invite Jesus to have a hard conversation with you about both lists.

Ask him how he wants to use those things on the first list to bring him honor and to enrich your life in the process.

Ask him to speak the truth to you about the second list.

Is there anything there that's partially true? Is there any part of what you've written that needs grit-fueled transformation from the inside out?

Now burn the second list. You don't need it; Jesus is on the case.

And Even Grittier

This will take a bit of planning. You'll need a full-length mirror and a great deal of privacy.

First, put the mirror in a place you won't—can't—be disturbed.

Second, strip naked.

Now look in the mirror and—out loud—describe what you see. When you're finished, keep reading.

We can wait...

All done? Here's what you did: You described every flaw you saw. Every wrinkle, sag, scar, and stretch mark. Because that's what we do. When we have frank conversations with ourselves, we're nearly always critical.

No wonder we so seldom have hard conversations with ourselves.

Now do this: Describe what *Jesus* sees when he looks at you. Who *Jesus* sees. How is his description different from yours?

•···•

What did you discover about how you view yourself?

_____

_____

What did you discover about how Jesus views you?

_____

_____

In what ways was this experience hard...and good?

_____

_____

Where was the spiritual grit in these experiences? How has Jesus used tough things to communicate his love for you?

_____

_____

Jesus had no problem having a hard conversation with Peter.

That's what love does. When it senses a rift in a relationship, it addresses it. When there's an untruth, love drags it out into the light to examine it.

Not harshly...but firmly.

Not out of anger...but because love doesn't do well in the darkness. It needs honesty and transparency. It breathes best in light, not shadow.

Do this: Read aloud this passage from Psalm 139:24: "Point out anything in me that offends you, and lead me along the path of everlasting life."

Now read it again, and mean it this time.

Listen and watch carefully for the next few days. What's Jesus pulling into the light for you to see?

What's the hard conversation he's wanting to have with you?

And Even Grittier

If you hear from Jesus, call another Jesus-follower and share what Jesus dragged into the light. Be honest.

Be transparent.

And be willing to have your friend pray with and for you.

What did these days of being open to a hard conversation with Jesus teach you about yourself?

_____

_____

What did you discover about Jesus?

_____

_____

In what ways was this experience hard...and good?

_____

_____

Where was the spiritual grit in these experiences? What freedom do you experience when Jesus moves something from darkness into light?

_____

_____

GRIT GROWER 37: PICK UP THE PHONE

This is going to sting a bit...but that's often the sensation of spiritual grit growing in you.

Ask Jesus who you need to have a hard conversation with. Who you need to call so you can say aloud what you've said so often in your thoughts:

Why did you hurt me? Why didn't you care? Do you know what your actions have cost me?

Hard conversations come in lots of flavors and sizes, but they have this in common: They're hard. They build grit.

And they can change everything.

You may not hear an apology. Any explanation might sound weak. That's okay—that builds grit, too.

Who's Jesus telling you to call? When will you do it?

And Even Grittier

Ask Jesus to bring to mind someone who'd benefit from having a hard conversation with *you*.

Someone *you've* hurt. Or abandoned. Or disappointed.

Someone who hasn't reached out to have a hard conversation about what you did or left undone.

Call that person, too.

Admit your failure. Say you're ready to hear whatever the person might want to tell you.

You might not agree with everything that's said, but you'll grow grit as you own whatever truth is laid in front of you.

And as you see the places Jesus still has work to do in you.

●┄┄┄┄┄┄┄┄┄┄┄┄┄┄┄┄┄┄┄┄┄┄┄┄┄┄┄┄┄┄┄┄┄┄┄┄┄●

What did you discover about yourself as you made these calls?

_____

_____

What did you discover about Jesus?

_____

_____

In what ways was this experience hard...and good?

_____

_____

Where was the spiritual grit in these experiences? Hurricanes stir up nutrients deep in the ocean, keeping them alive. How has a hard conversation brought new life into your story?

_____

_____

SPIRITUAL GRIT MEETS...
WALKING AWAY

John works with at-risk teenagers.

Sex offenders, gang members, arsonists, drug users—John sees them all. If a teenager gets sideways with the justice system in his community, it's likely John will sit down with the kid for a conversation.

And those conversations seldom go well.

"When kids come to our program because a probation officer ordered it," John says, "that's not the best way to start a relationship."

No matter what else he's helping kids deal with, John wants to support them as they address their addictions—especially if they're on drugs.

"The problem is, it doesn't matter if I tell a kid to get clean. Until teenagers *want* to be off drugs, they can't do it."

But day after day, John gives it a try. He has hard conversation after hard conversation.

A harder conversation is when John tells a teenager to leave the program. To get out...now.

"When a kid has proven he's not ready to change, I've got to cut him loose—even if I'm sending him back to detention or the streets. I've got to make room for a kid who might be willing to change."

Those are hard, grit-growing conversations.

And harder still are conversations John has with teenagers he's asked to leave who say they've seen the light and want back into the program. Who ask John to trust them after they've shown again and again they couldn't be trusted.

"These are kids who threw away everything we did for them. Some literally spit in my face as they stormed out, cursing me over their shoulders.

"But when they're serious about coming back, they need to know I'll be there for them."

Tough situation. Tough conversations. Gritty all around.

But John knows what to do because he's had the same hard conversations himself...with Jesus.

"I've stepped away from Jesus many, many times...and he's let me go. But he's never walked away from me, and he's never failed to welcome me home when I come back to him," says John.

GIVE UP ON GETTING EVEN

James and John are *ticked*.

Things are already tense; Jesus and his disciples are on their way to Jerusalem, unsure how they'll be received. And as the group travels through Samaria, Jesus sends messengers ahead to a village so they're ready to take care of him and his crew.

But Jesus isn't welcome there, not if he's on his way to Jerusalem. Apparently the bitterness Samaritans harbor toward Jews includes Jesus and the disciples.

Yet again in Jesus' life, there's going to be no room in the inn.

James and John urge Jesus to go full Sodom and Gomorrah on the village, calling down fire from heaven to teach the inhospitable Samaritans a lesson they'll never forget, assuming they live through it at all.

Jesus not only doesn't do as they want, but Luke reports, "Jesus turned and rebuked them" (Luke 9:55). Some early manuscripts add, "For the Son of Man has not come to destroy people's lives, but to save them."

So much for James and John evening the score with the Samaritans.*

James and John aren't the only ones keeping score and getting even—we do it, too. And let's admit it: It feels good. We applaud when bad guys get what they deserve.

But getting even isn't something Jesus has ever delegated to his disciples. Not to James and John, and not to us. Someone else will make sure evildoers face the consequences of their actions. That's covered without our help.

And there's the tension where spiritual grit is built: choosing to give up on getting even.

Choosing to tear up the score card and walk away from demanding justice.

That's hard stuff—especially when you have the power to get even or, perhaps, impose a little punishment. Holding your fire when righteous indignation is pushing you to pull the trigger is remarkably difficult.

And the very thing Jesus does daily.

Because, while he loves those Samaritans in the village ahead, they *are* rejecting him. And while he loves the disciples sauntering along beside him, it's *their* sins that are taking him to the cross.

Jesus has given up on getting even so he can grab hold of something else: forgiveness.

The good news for the Samaritan villagers was this: James and John didn't have the power to call down fire from heaven. Had that been possible, the village would have been a smoking crater within minutes.

And here's the good news for you: While Jesus *does* have the power to direct fire and brimstone your way, he's offering you something else.

Something just as powerful but far more redemptive.

He's offering you forgiveness.

Read the entire account in Luke 9:51-56.

GRIT GROWER 38: HOLD YOUR FIRE

There was a time getting even required squaring off for a duel, or at least a fistfight.

But that's so last century.

Now we've got the internet.

You simply find someone's social media account and post a scathing review. You describe in detail what the person did and destroy a reputation. You can make accusations anonymously. You can take your best shot and then walk away.

But that's not what disciples do.

Disciples follow Jesus...and he didn't take revenge.

Do this: Find a social media account of someone who's hurt you. Look at the happy faces in the photos posted there. Read the list of accomplishments, and notice how carefully the public persona has been cultivated.

Now imagine what you could write to set the record straight.

And don't do it. Instead, hold your fire.

Walk away.

And Even Grittier

Jesus said, "Bless those who curse you. Pray for those who hurt you" (Luke 6:28).

That's going one better than simply not taking revenge. It's being loving toward people you prefer to hate.

But you're a disciple who's following Jesus. You're on a path that led him to pray from the cross for the very people who were torturing him.

That's grit...and that's who you follow.

Why would you think he'd lead you anywhere but where he's gone himself?

That person whose indifference or anger has hurt you?

Pray for that person.

•···•

What did you discover about yourself from these experiences?

_____

_____

How is what you just did like or unlike something Jesus has done?

_____

_____

Where was the spiritual grit in these experiences? What is scary or uncomfortable about letting go of a past hurt, and why?

_____

_____

> **"Dear friends, never take revenge. Leave that to the righteous anger of God. For the Scriptures say, 'I will take revenge; I will pay them back,' says the Lord"**
> **(Romans 12:19).**

GRIT GROWER 39: STOP KEEPING SCORE

Take a wooden pencil and a piece of paper to a quiet spot where you can think and write without being disturbed.

On the paper list wrongs that have been done to you.

Not all of them—just those that have echoed through your life awhile. Abuse. Adultery. Betrayal. Cheating. Lies that cost you dearly.

Be specific and detailed. Name names—you won't be showing this to anyone.

When you've finished (or run out of paper) read your list aloud. Let any feelings that come wash over and through you.

Invite Jesus to see your list through your eyes, eyes that may be filled with tears.

Ask him to help you see through his eyes, too. Sorrowful eyes that hold a spark of hope.

Then tear the paper into tiny pieces and snap the pencil in half.

You may not be ready to forgive yet—that's between you and Jesus. But you can decide to quit keeping score.

You can take a step toward trusting that God will make right what others made wrong.

And Even Grittier

Go someplace you can see a scoreboard. A local football or soccer field, a community gym, maybe even a bowling alley.

Once you're there, get comfortable and look long and hard at that scoreboard.

Ask Jesus this question: *When it comes to my getting even with others, what's the score?*

Expect to hear...nothing.

Because Jesus isn't big on your keeping score. He's way more interested in your discovering how to let him fuel your ability to forgive others.

So then ask him this question: *What needs to change in me so I won't worry about the score at all?*

You can expect he'll have a *lot* to say to you about that.

●··●

What did you discover about yourself from these experiences?

_____

_____

How did what you just did remind you of what Jesus has done?

_____

_____

In what ways was this experience hard...and good?

_____

_____

Where was the spiritual grit in these experiences?

_____

_____

GRIT GROWER 40: COUNT THE COST

In the movies it usually looks like this: The hero finally has the bad guy cornered, finally has a gun aimed squarely at the bad guy's forehead.

A partner, priest, or compadre says, "Don't do it. Don't pull the trigger. If you do, you're no better than him."

A dramatic pause, and then the bad guy's life is spared. Roll credits.

There's some wisdom there.

Do you really want to be someone who repays evil with evil? someone who wants to ask Jesus to look the other way for a few minutes while you take care of business and get your revenge?

No. You don't.

Well, maybe you *do*...but that's not the direction Jesus is leading you.

Do this today: Ask Jesus to give you a heart that's willing to give up on getting even. You'll need his help because it's not natural to walk away from revenge. It takes a power that comes from beyond yourself.

It takes power from him.

Seriously: Pray for that heart. Sooner or later, you're going to need it.

And Even Grittier

Sit with a trusted friend who's also a follower of Jesus, and tell that person about you and getting even. About whether you're careful to keep score and settle up or you never even think about getting even.

And share what your approach to keeping score costs you. Do you find yourself quick to strike back and feel guilty later? Do you refuse to get even but find your stomach churning whenever you see someone who took advantage of you?

Reveal who you are...and who you need to forgive and why. Ask your friend to pray for you.

And offer to pray for your friend, too.

•···•

What did you discover about yourself as you prayed?

_____

_____

What did you discover about Jesus?

_____

_____

In what ways was this experience hard...and good?

_____

_____

Where was the spiritual grit in these experiences? How does holding on to past hurts affect your ability to be vulnerable in relationships, and why?

_____

_____

GRIT GROWER 4I: A SCORE-SETTLING SCORE

Fire up your laptop or tablet and find some streaming music sites.

Your challenge: Find a song that captures how you feel about walking away from settling a score.

Maybe the thought of letting someone get away with something angers you. It seems so very unfair.

Or it disappoints you—you've been looking forward to payback.

Perhaps not getting revenge makes you happy, frightened, or something else.

Whatever you feel, find a song that reflects that feeling.

Play it—loud.

If it has lyrics, sing along.

This is the soundtrack of your life at the moment...and a way to tell Jesus how you're feeling.

And Even Grittier

Field trip time again: This time to a cemetery.

Find the oldest section and walk among the headstones.

Notice the names. Do the math as you read the dates of births and deaths; consider lives lived and lives cut short.

So many people.

And none of them care any longer about who once angered them or who owed them a coin, compliment, or consideration.

That list of debts was erased on the last day carved on each tombstone. Getting even no longer mattered.

A thought: If death can erase the need to get even, how might something a bit less lethal do the same thing? How might forgiveness? How might love?

Ask Jesus what it's costing you to carry around your list of paybacks and what he'd have you do with it.

•...•

What did you discover about yourself as you considered getting even?

_____

_____

What did you discover about Jesus?

_____

_____

In what ways was this experience hard...and good?

_____

_____

Where was the spiritual grit in these experiences?

_____

_____

SPIRITUAL GRIT MEETS...
THE LADY ON THE AISLE

Denise wanted to kill the woman.

But on the long list of things flight attendants can't do to cranky flyers, murder ranks right up there.

And so does getting even.

The whole thing started when Denise was passing through the cabin, trash bag in hand, collecting leftover food containers and plastic cups.

"I usually reach over to a middle or window seat to take what people are holding," Denise explains. "But if you're seated on the aisle, I assume you can just drop your trash in the bag because it's right there."

A woman seated on the aisle took exception to Denise's system.

"She assumed I was refusing to give her the same service I gave her seatmates," says Denise.

When the woman complained, Denise apologized, explained her system, and offered to take the woman's trash.

"She refused," says Denise. "Instead, she waited until I passed by and then dropped her trash in the aisle so I'd have to pick it up. When I saw what she'd done, she made eye contact, smiled sweetly, and then resumed flipping through her magazine.

"She must have thought there was nothing I could do."

She was wrong.

Flight attendants usually have the complete support not only of one another, but of the captains as well. Which means being belligerent with Denise could have earned the passenger anything from a humiliating lecture from the captain to being denied access to her connecting flight.

Denise could have made the woman's life difficult but chose to do nothing.

Except pick up the trash.

"I took a few deep breaths to calm myself down and then quietly told the passenger I was disappointed in her behavior. I told her she was better than this.

"And even if she wasn't, because of Jesus, I was."

DON'T WORRY

When Jesus tells a crowd—one that includes his disciples—not to worry, they wonder if he's forgotten who he's talking to. Because, from where they sit, they're dealing with a few worry-worthy issues in life.

For starters, most of them are poor.

That whole "Give us this day our daily bread" request Jesus tucks into his model prayer is real; many people shuffling around in Jesus' audience are literally unsure where their next meal will come from.

Which explains one reason there's such excitement whenever Jesus multiplies fish and bread and provides an all-you-can-eat buffet.

Plus, there's this: Their future is shaky at best.

The Jewish people in Jesus' audience are never sure what might set off the Roman soldiers patrolling their neighborhoods. One wrong look, one cross word, a misunderstanding of any sort—the Romans have no shortage of crosses they can pull out on a moment's notice.

Still, Jesus says this:

"You cannot serve God and be enslaved to money.

"That is why I tell you not to worry about everyday life—whether you have enough food and drink, or enough clothes to wear.

"Isn't life more than food, and your body more than clothing?

"Look at the birds. They don't plant or harvest or store food in barns, for your heavenly Father feeds them. And aren't you far more valuable to him than they are?

"Can all your worries add a single moment to your life?" (Matthew 6:24-27).

Great advice, Jesus...but it's hard not to think about money when you're worried about feeding your family. If Jesus would multiply some silver coins instead of bread, a great deal of worry would evaporate instantly.

Besides, worrying is what some of us do best.

Fast forward and Jesus is sending his 12 disciples out into the world to do ministry. And he's allowing them to take with them...nothing.

No money. No food. No clothes other than what's on their backs.

All they get is a walking stick—period.

Once again, it seems Jesus is deliberately allowing a worrisome situation to continue. What's he up to?

Perhaps this: Spiritual grit grows when his disciples find themselves forced to rely on him rather than themselves. As positive as self-reliance can be, it's not the point of spiritual grit. In fact, it can seriously undermine it.

Spiritually gritty people rely on Jesus, not themselves. The strength and character they develop serves them well, but it never pulls their eyes off Jesus.

Jesus' first disciples discovered that truth, and it's waiting for the rest of us Jesus-followers to discover, too. You included.

The ability to not worry doesn't come from being so strong that nothing can harm you. You'll never be that strong. Rather, it comes from following someone else who's so strong that you can never be separated from him and the eternal life he offers you.

When you're with Jesus, you never have to worry.

Because you're with Jesus.

Read the entire account in Matthew 6:19-34.

GRIT GROWER 42: TELL A FRIEND

Tell a friend what you worry about most.

Is it money? health? relationships? What pegs your worry meter, and what do you think drives that worry?

Have the conversation, and then ask your friend to pray for you. Right now, not later.

And out loud so you can hear what God's hearing. So you can soak up the encouragement that comes with knowing God is aware of what's worrying you.

And Even Grittier

Get thee to a waiting room.

At the Department of Motor Vehicles, a pharmacy, or a hospital. Anywhere you're not required to sign in and can sit without being booted out.

Then...wait.

Wait for five minutes...then ten...wait an hour if you want. Nothing will happen. You won't be called to the counter; your number will never appear on the monitor.

And that's exactly what you're doing when you worry: You're waiting for something that may not happen.

While you're waiting, invite Jesus to sit with you.

Maybe there's something he wants to say to you about worry.

•···•

What did you discover about yourself as you considered worry? as your friend prayed for you?

_____

_____

What did you discover about Jesus?

_____

_____

In what ways was this experience hard...and good?

_____

_____

Where was the spiritual grit in these experiences?

_____

_____

GRIT GROWER 43: FIVE-MINUTE BAG

Use an old backpack or suitcase to create a five-minute bag.

That's the bag you'd grab if you got word you had five minutes to evacuate your house or apartment. If a fire was sweeping closer or a flood washing your way, it's the stuff that will help you reclaim your life later.

Medications. Insurance policies. Your birth certificate and passport. A thumb drive loaded with family photos, documents, and electronic records. Food and water for a couple of days. Spare batteries.

A Bible.

Whatever you'd take, bag it now.

Keeping that bag tucked behind a closet door, ready to grab and go, is one way to reduce worry. But it doesn't stop the fire or the flood from coming. It doesn't replace what will really tame your worry: *trusting Jesus*.

By the way, having a five-minute bag isn't a bad idea, so make one.

But ask Jesus about trusting him more, too. What does he suggest about trusting him more...so you can worry less?

And Even Grittier

Poke a hole in the center of a piece of notebook paper.

Now take your newly created view blocker with you and meet a friend for coffee, preferably someplace where there's a lot going on.

Starbucks, maybe. Or a sidewalk café.

Hold the paper up so you can peer, one-eyed, through the hole as you talk.

Carry on a conversation for a few minutes before dropping the paper. Notice that, as you talked with your friend, you didn't notice the stares of other patrons who are clearly looking at you now.

Narrowing your focus to just your friend helped you not notice anything—or anyone—else.

Was that a good thing? Less than good?

And how's that like paying ridiculous attention to Jesus and not paying attention to those things that prompt you to worry?

By the way, you've got a *wonderfully* patient friend. You should definitely pick up the check. Definitely.

●..●

What did you discover about yourself as you considered worry in your life?

What did you discover about Jesus?

In what ways was this experience hard...and good?

Where was the spiritual grit in these experiences? What are some things you do that unnecessarily contribute to your anxiety, and what can you do about them?

GRIT GROWER 44: BUBBLE WRAP

Do this: Use bubble wrap to encase the most important item in your home.

It can be anything, or anyone, as long as it's precious to you.

Step back to admire your work.

Invite Jesus to stand at your elbow and take a look, too.

A question: How much do you worry about harm coming to what's precious to you? Does that worry peg your emotional Richter scale, or doesn't it cross your mind?

And how much do you worry about harm coming to your relationships—especially your friendship with Jesus? What do you do to protect that friendship?

There's no need to worry about Jesus drifting away from your friendship. He's all-in—always.

So abide. Just abide.

Remain connected to Jesus, and he'll give you the grit to abide in him.

And Even Grittier

Give something away—something you worry you might lose one day.

A family heirloom...that high school sports trophy you can't bear to throw out...a refinished piece of furniture that proves you're the undisputed DIY Champion of the Universe.

Whatever it is, however significant it is to you, hand it to a friend who's long admired it...or drop it into a Goodwill bin.

Hard to even contemplate, isn't it?

But the truth is, no amount of worry makes your treasure yours forever. Or protects it from all that can harm it. There's no true security other than the security you'll find in Jesus, and he's way more interested in people than he is in your coin collection.

So...will you do it?

•..•

What did you discover about yourself as you pondered worry and trust?

_____

_____

What did you discover about Jesus?

_____

_____

In what ways was this experience hard...and good?

_____

_____

Where was the spiritual grit in these experiences?

_____

_____

GRIT GROWER 45: WORRIES, DISSECTED

Dissect one worry that's keeping you up at night. Break it down into smaller pieces.

That lump you've felt? The one you fear might be the beginning of your end?

It needs to be checked out, so make a list:

• Call your doctor.
• Set an appointment.
• Get test results, and then decide on next steps.

Worries grow strong in the absence of action. And they grow stronger still when you don't invite Jesus into the situations that worry you.

Because look at each of those steps above.

Which one is bigger or more powerful than Jesus?

None. So don't face your worries alone. Take Jesus along.

He has the grit to stick with you and the power to fix what's broken.

And Even Grittier

Light up a room.

Really light it—drag in lamps from all over the house. Open up the drapes and throw wide the shutters. Even flip on that flashlight you keep in the junk drawer.

Then jot on a sheet of paper the worry you told your friend about (Grit Grower 42). Lay that paper on the floor, and aim as much light as possible directly at it.

Ask Jesus to look at the worry you wrote down.

That should be easy because you've lit it well enough to be visible from space and he's considerably closer than that.

Then ask Jesus to flood your heart with peace, just as you've flooded the room with light. To remove worry from your heart and mind even if the situation prompting that worry isn't resolved.

To replace worry with trust.

And amen.

•···•

What did you discover about yourself through these experiences?

_____

_____

What did you discover about Jesus?

_____

_____

In what ways were these experiences hard...and good?

_____

_____

Where was the spiritual grit in these experiences?

_____

_____

Back in the day, Grandpa Jack bought a new Buick every five years.

Buicks were perfect old-guy cars because they were the size of living rooms and floated over rough roads without a tremor.

And Grandpa Jack, who was Russ' grandfather, kept his Buick in showroom condition.

"He washed his car every Saturday morning even if he hadn't pulled it out of the garage all week," says Russ.

Russ tagged along once when Grandpa Jack went car shopping.

"He walked into the dealership with a description of the car he wanted in one hand and his checkbook in the other. He announced that he expected to buy the car—outright—that was described on his list.

"And he expected to pay the amount he'd filled out on a check. Whoever could make that happen would have a sale that day.

"No haggling. No delays. No upsells. Cash on the barrel—that was Grandpa Jack."

Because Jack had calculated a reasonable price, within an hour a shiny new Buick was sitting in front of the dealership, ready for him to drive away.

Russ, having just gotten his driver's license, was supposed to drive the old Buick home. But before he took off, Grandpa Jack asked him to retrieve a hammer from the trunk.

Russ did as he was asked and handed over the hammer.

"The salesman and I watched Grandpa Jack walk behind the new Buick and carefully smack the bumper—hard—on the temporary license plate. He then lifted the paper, examined the small dent he'd made, and nodded in satisfaction."

Russ says he and the salesman thought Grandpa Jack had lost his mind and told him so.

"Grandpa Jack said that now he didn't need to worry about who might put the first dent in his new car," Russ says. "He knew who'd done it. It was him."

When Russ got the old Buick home, he carefully lifted the metal license plate and sure enough: There was a small dent.

One about as big around as a hammer tap and as deep as a new car owner's peace of mind.

That hard thing dreaded by most new car owners—the appearance of a first dent or ding—held no power over Grandpa Jack.

Knowing the secret under his license plate allowed Grandpa Jack to relax.

Knowing who you follow and who loves you—let that help you relax, too.

LET PEOPLE KNOW YOU'RE WITH JESUS

In the end, Jesus' first disciples decide to run away rather than admit they know him.

Hearts pounding, shame coursing through them, they hide their faces. Keep to the shadows. Anything to avoid following Jesus to the cross.

Even Peter—loyal-to-a-fault Peter—swears by all that's holy he doesn't know Jesus, has never met the man being brutally beaten in the high priest's house.

Peter bolts, leaving both Jesus and his self-respect behind.

And even as Peter abandons Jesus, his master's words ring in his ears. Only a few hours ago, Jesus leaned forward at their shared Passover meal, telling his disciples this:

"And you must also testify about me because you have been with me from the beginning of my ministry" (John 15:27).

Testify?

The dozen disciples can't even be *located*. They're hiding in the darkest corner of Jerusalem they can find.

But what choice do they have? In the days following Jesus' crucifixion, being associated with him is risking being labeled a heretic, perhaps an enemy of the state. Either accusation can prove fatal.*

In some parts of the world, the same risk remains today: Taking a public stand for Jesus can cost you your life.

And yet Jesus insists that those who follow him do so openly, not as secret admirers but in full view. As Jesus was prepping his closest disciples for a short-term mission trip, he said this to them:

"Everyone who acknowledges me publicly here on earth, I will also acknowledge before my Father in heaven. But everyone who denies me here on earth, I will also deny before my Father in heaven" (Matthew 10:32-33).

In other words, no traveling incognito. Jesus' disciples were to clearly associate themselves with him as they healed and worked in his name.

If you happen to be a missionary serving in a society where open identification with Jesus will get you beheaded, let's assume you get a pass on this. You *are* openly identifying with Jesus; just doing so one trusted person at a time.

But for the rest of us, Jesus' demand might be awkward.

Yes, we follow him...but we aren't sure we want everyone to know. Christians as a tribe have a difficult reputation: We're often viewed as narrow-minded, intolerant, hypocritical, and homophobic. Do you really want to plaster that sort of label on your chest? It may be wrong, it may be a stereotype, but it's believed nonetheless.

Odd, isn't it? Everyone talks about the spiritual grit required to have a personal relationship with Jesus, but it's living out a *public* relationship with him that can get you killed. Or at least make you uncomfortable.

Yet Jesus insists we acknowledge him—and with more than bumper stickers and T-shirts. He's looking for us to stand up for him not only with words but also with actions.

That's what he's done—and is doing—for us.

How can we do less for him?

It's a classic question that's been asked of Jesus-followers for generations: If you were put on trial for following Jesus, would there be enough evidence to convict you?

That question is usually trotted out as a hammer, meant to smack an audience into doing more, saying more, giving more.

But intent aside, it's actually a fair question.

Jesus asks you to acknowledge him—to remove any doubt about your allegiance to him. To state clearly who he is in your life.

If that's happening, it's going to leave some evidence in its wake.

Not just words, but lives touched.

Not just good intentions, but actions taken.

So picture asking Jesus that question: *If I were put on trial for following you, would there be enough evidence to convict me?*

And what might he say if he were called to the stand to testify on your behalf?

*Read the entire account in Matthew 26:47-75.

GRIT GROWER 46: TAKE A STAND

If it's election season, put a sign in your yard or window declaring your preference for a certain candidate or issue.

And election season or not, fire up social media and link to a church site or another Christian site.

Take a stand.

Go public.

In whatever way Jesus leads you, get off the bench and into the game.

See what happens.

And Even Grittier

Go stand alongside Jesus.

Do it at an institution in your community you think has turned its back on Jesus.

Maybe it's a strip club. A government office. Or a church whose theology you question. Go stand anywhere you, judging as lovingly as you can, believe has given up on Jesus.

Stand in the shadow of that place and quietly ask Jesus to be with the people who are in its circle of influence.

Be legal—stand on the sidewalk or other place open to the public. And don't take along bullhorns, bombast, or signs. They won't be welcome, and you don't need them.

Not to pray. Not to quietly stand with Jesus.

By the way, you can be sure he's there because no matter how thoroughly people walk away from him, he doesn't walk away from them.

And if you were wrong? If the organization also honors Jesus and you just don't know it?

He's still there.

Either way, you're standing with him.

•···•

What did you discover about yourself as you considered taking a public stand for Jesus?

_____

_____

What did you discover about Jesus as you asked him about taking a stand?

_____

_____

In what ways was this experience hard...and good?

_____

_____

Where was the spiritual grit in these experiences?

_____

_____

GRIT GROWER 47: SAY IT WITH CHALK

Buy sidewalk chalk, and in front of where you live, draw the following on the sidewalk or street:

"Someone who loves Jesus lives here."

You won't get in trouble for vandalism: One rainstorm or hosing will wash away the chalk. And in many places in the world, you won't get in trouble for sharing what you believe: Free speech is a wonderful thing.

Still...how does it feel being that bold about your faith? to be so clear about who you are and whose you are?

And Even Grittier

Someone famously said, "Preach the gospel at all times and when necessary use words."

That's your grit-growing challenge: Treat others in such a way today that they're prompted to ask what's different about you, what's fueling your kindness, compassion, and empathy.

When they ask, tell them: You're following Jesus.

What did you discover about yourself as you declared your connection to Jesus?

What did you discover about Jesus?

In what ways was this experience hard...and good?

_____

_____

Where was the spiritual grit in these experiences?

_____

_____

GRIT GROWER 48: AMBASSADOR YOU

Write "Ambassador" on a piece of paper, and tape it to whatever mirror you use to make yourself presentable in the morning.

See your face above the word tomorrow morning, the next morning, all week.

You're seeing yourself for who you are: an all-in, sold-out representative of Jesus.

As a follower of Jesus, you've been appointed to represent him in your corner of the world.

He's expecting you to live as he lives. To trust whom he trusts. To represent him to the best of your abilities. To fly his flag and show what life is like in your home country, which, in your case, is heaven.

Do you do that perfectly? No...but no ambassador does it perfectly.

Perfection isn't possible, but faithfully identifying with Jesus is.

So fly the flag. Be faithful.

And Even Grittier

Make an "Ambassador" name plate, and display it where others can see it.

If you're at work, slide a piece of paper with "Ambassador" printed on it over that lame name plate they gave you. At home you can tape it to the front door.

Trust us: When others see your sign, you'll be asked about it.

When that happens, explain you're a Jesus-follower and why that qualifies you to be an ambassador.

By the way, if someone asks you to stamp her passport, tell her how to get to heaven.

•···•

What did you discover about yourself as you began thinking of yourself as an ambassador for Jesus?

_____

_____

What did you discover about Jesus?

_____

_____

In what ways was this experience hard...and good?

_____

_____

Where was the spiritual grit in these experiences? How would others say you represent Jesus well?

_____

_____

SPIRITUAL GRIT MEETS...
THE SUBWAY

There's a rule every subway commuter learns fast: Don't react.

Not to the drunk sleeping it off, slumped in the corner seat.

Not to the angry couple sitting cross-armed and scowling at the front of the car.

And not to what people are reading as they tunnel into paperbacks or their tablets to avoid having a conversation with you.

"Deb and I were headed downtown to the St. Andrew Station to catch a movie," Kevin remembers of one memorable trip on the Toronto Subway. "Deb noticed that the man next to us was reading a battered copy of Fritz Ridenour's *How to be a Christian Without Being Religious.*

"Deb elbowed me and whispered that I should tell him I was a Christian and knew how to do that. You know, stand up for Jesus and see what happened."

But Kevin knew the rules, and interrupting someone to talk about faith broke most of them.

Besides, Kevin didn't want to come off as some sort of Christian zealot. The guy was minding his own business; shouldn't he and Deb do the same?

It took three applications of Deb's elbow before Kevin got the man's attention. And it took about 20 seconds for the man to begin sharing his story.

He'd left a dying church but still liked Jesus. He was wondering if he could follow Jesus on his own or if that was a hopeless cause.

"That led to an intense conversation," says Kevin. The three passengers decided to forget what they'd planned and to get coffee instead.

"We talked for two hours and invited him to a church that *wasn't* dead—our church. He was there the next Sunday and has been coming ever since.

"I'm thinking Jesus set up that encounter," says Kevin. "The book, our seats on the subway, Deb's elbows—all of it."

BE UNIFIED

When Jesus prays that his followers find unity, the disciples aren't surprised. Jesus has been pushing them to get along for years, ever since he called them to follow him.

Because really, the only thing the disciples have in common is Jesus.

Some of them knew each other before Jesus recruited them. James and John are brothers, as are Peter and Andrew. But anyone who's been raised with a brother will tell you that doesn't always mean you're unified.

Sometimes brothers are the *least* united people you're likely to find.

And the other disciples Jesus throws together? He couldn't pick less likely people to call to unity.

Take Matthew and Simon the Zealot.

Matthew's a tax collector. Was one, anyway, before quitting to come with Jesus.

He worked for the Romans and, with a soldier or two at his side, made sure his neighbors handed over their fair share of taxes to Rome. Their fair share and perhaps a bit more to line his own pockets.

And Simon? He's a zealot, a member of one of the nationalist groups dedicated to evicting, killing, or maiming as many Romans—and Jews who've sold out to Rome—as possible.

Jesus recruits both men...and then has them travel together. Two men who previously wouldn't consider being in the same room are expected to work alongside each other and to be more than colleagues. They're to become brothers in the best, kingdom sense of the word.

It's not listed as a miracle, but Matthew and Simon heading off side by side and then both coming back alive? That's right up there with water into wine.

Jesus values unity so highly that, just hours before he's arrested, he prays this for his disciples:

"I pray that they will all be one, just as you and I are one—as you are in me, Father, and I am in you. And may they be in us so that the world will believe you sent me...May they experience such perfect unity that the world will know that you sent me and that you love them as much as you love me" (John 17:21, 23).

Clearly, unity is important to Jesus. But why?

Because it signals to the world that Jesus is legit. The change that happens in his disciples proves there's power in their passion for Jesus.

Besides, Jesus has ever and always been about relationships. He's calling his disciples not only to himself but also to one another. His kingdom isn't only about a new order but also a new way for God and people to connect, and for people to connect with one another.*

And then there's this: Relationships are a great place for grit to grow. They require listening. Compassion. Forgiveness. Grit-growers, all.

Relationships are challenging, calling out the best in you and revealing your worst.

And they pave the way, ultimately, to a unity that reflects the relationship Jesus has with the Father and the Holy Spirit. *That's* what real unity looks like when it's all grown up.

Is getting there hard? Ask Matthew and Simon—they'll tell you.

Unity takes having a passion for Jesus that's so strong it accepts who he accepts. Serves those he serves. It takes letting Jesus teach you to soften your heart and hold your tongue.

And is it worth the effort?

Ask Jesus.

Read the entire account in John 17:1-26.

GRIT GROWER 49: NEIGHBORHOOD DIRECTORY

One way to build unity is to connect people who live near one another, people who live in your apartment block, say, or whose houses line your street.

Go knock on doors and explain that you're assembling a neighborhood directory, one that will help neighbors get to know one another better.

Give each neighbor a copy of your directory information, already filled out: name, address, phone number, email, hobbies, any odd jobs you do for fun or money, and a few lines explaining where you're from and how long you've lived where you live.

Ask each neighbor to fill out a similar sheet for the directory, and promise to give a directory to each one after you've completed it.

Congratulations: You've met your neighbors. And helped build unity. Plus, you now know where all the potential babysitters live.

And Even Grittier

Invite your neighbors to a hot dog roast—at your place.

Get your hands on a portable fire pit, and park it out front where everyone can see it. Then go buy enough drinks, hot dogs, buns, and condiments to feed the masses. And snag some wire hangers, too—you'll need plenty for heating hot dogs.

Invite your neighbors in advance and ask for an RSVP.

Point out this is a tasty way to connect with people who live nearby but might as well live on another planet insofar as conversations are concerned.

Make it fun: music, laughter, games for the kids.

And hot dogs. Lots and lots of hot dogs.

What did you discover about yourself—and your neighbors?

_____

_____

How might Jesus suggest you invest in these new relationships? What did he say when you asked him?

_____

_____

In what ways was this experience hard...and good?

_____

_____

Where was the spiritual grit in these experiences?

_____

_____

GRIT GROWER 50: UNCOMMON COMMONALITIES; COMMON UNCOMMONALITIES

You'll need another Jesus-follower for this, so call someone you know only marginally. A friend of a friend. That person who's new to church. Just make sure it's not an old friend you already know well.

All set?

Perfect! Do this: Take three minutes to identify as many things as possible that the two of you have in common. Not the obvious stuff (you both have noses) but things that are a bit deeper (you both love the smell of coffee).

Three minutes. See how much you have in common.

Now take three minutes to identify your differences. Political parties, food preferences, favorite Bible translations.

Then discuss this: In what ways does your shared belief in Jesus unite the two of you? Does that shared belief trump the differences you identified?

Why—or why not?

And Even Grittier

This is going to be fun. It may ding your dignity a bit, but it'll be worth it.

Buy a bottle of bubbles—the kind that come with a wand.

Recruit a friend to sit with you on a park bench and take turns blowing bubbles. Lots of bubbles. Offer passersby opportunities to give it a try, too, especially people who look like they could use some cheering up.

And small kids. Small kids *love* bubbles.

Run that bottle right down until you've got nothing but fumes in it. Then talk about this: How has this experience affected your friendship? Do you feel closer to this friend...or more distant?

We're betting the experience further cements your friendship, that you'll enjoy this memory together for years.

What's true with your bubble buddy is also true with Jesus: When you have an adventure with him—even a silly one—you grow closer to him.

And your friendship with Jesus is ultimately your best—and only—source of spiritual grit.

What adventures have you shared with Jesus lately?

Up for one?

•⋯⋯⋯⋯⋯⋯⋯⋯⋯⋯⋯⋯⋯⋯⋯⋯⋯⋯⋯⋯⋯⋯•

What did you discover about yourself through these experiences?

_____

_____

What did you discover about Jesus?

_____

_____

In what ways was this experience hard...and good?

_____

_____

Where was the spiritual grit in these experiences?

_____

_____

GRIT GROWER 51: BUILD UNITY

You'll need a pad of sticky notes and a pen...plus a desire to transform those notes into unity-builders.

Do this: Carry the pad with you throughout your day. Look for opportunities to build unity by inserting a dose of encouragement into the lives of friends, family members, and strangers.

When people feel appreciated and confident, they're far more open to noticing others. To new ideas. To doing all the stuff that builds unity and strengthens relationships.

Stick encouraging notes on the doors of neighbors. Leave notes around the office for co-workers to find. Stick them in books when you're at the library. Pop them in your child's lunchbox, in the book bag of your spouse or friend.

Find ways to say, "You're appreciated. You're making a difference. The world's a better place because you're in it."

Build some unity today.

And Even Grittier

Ask people for help.

Nothing builds unity more quickly than asking for and gratefully receiving advice.

How to navigate a computer program. The best Chinese restaurant on this side of town. The recipe for those incredible brownies Marge brought to work.

Build bridges with others by valuing what they know or can do.

Start small...or maybe dive deep.

Ask how someone else is dealing with an issue that's also hounding you.

Ask—and listen. Carefully. Humbly.

You're building unity and growing grit as, together, you and Jesus sift through the advice you hear.

What did you discover about yourself through these unity experiences?

_____

_____

In what ways is what you did like what Jesus does in the world... sometimes through his followers?

_____

_____

In what ways was this experience hard...and good?

_____

_____

Where was the spiritual grit in these experiences? From your perspective, what is blocking greater unity in the world today?

_____

_____

GRIT GROWER 52: LOSE THE PHONE, PAL

Put your phone away.

Don't use it to distract yourself as you stand in line, make the commute, or fill spare moments. Instead, look up and smile.

Make contact with the people around you.

Risk striking up a conversation.

See what you have in common with the rest of humanity. And as you interact, keep an ear cocked for Jesus' whisper letting you know how you might serve or bless someone.

That listening you're doing?

It's focusing on Jesus. Abiding in him. Building grit.

And Even Grittier

What most people think of as listening is just waiting for the chance to talk.

Listening—*really* listening—is an act of unity. Always. Every time.

So today sit down with someone and do the hard work of listening. Of hearing what she's saying and noticing how she's feeling. Of asking follow-up questions to give her the space to explore her story more deeply.

You're giving her a rare and priceless gift: your complete attention.

She's giving you an equally valuable thing: She's sharing her life.

Ask Jesus who he wants you to listen to today.

Then see what it takes to make it happen.

•··•

What did you discover about yourself as a listener?

_____

_____

What did you discover about Jesus as a listener?

_____

_____

In what ways was this experience hard...and good?

_____

_____

Where was the spiritual grit in these experiences?

_____

_____

SPIRITUAL GRIT MEETS... THE MARINES

When Adam joined the Marines, he knew he'd face some challenges.

He now admits that, even having done his homework, he had no idea what lay ahead.

Thirteen weeks of beyond-exhausted, high-stress, constant-friction, no-excuses, round-the-clock training that stretched Adam physically, mentally, and emotionally. That tore him down to atoms and rebuilt him as something he came to recognize in the mirror as a United States Marine.

And a rock-solid belief that fellow Marines were more than just people in the same job; they were a unified, in-sync band of brothers and sisters.

"That's something preached nonstop in boot camp," says Adam. "Unit cohesion and teamwork are right up there with physical fitness and marksmanship.

"You hear that the Marines around you may save your life," says Adam, "And once I was deployed, I found that to be absolutely true."

Adam is uncomfortable sharing details, but he does say that when his unit came under enemy fire, he realized for the first time there was no difference between himself and any of the men around him.

They were no longer white, Latino, or black.

Accents didn't matter. Religious and political affiliations didn't matter. Who'd made rank first didn't matter.

They were Marines united in purpose: to hurt the enemy, to survive, and to help the Marines next to them survive.

"I don't know that I've ever felt that connected to anyone else," says Adam.

"That's when you know that all the boot camp pain and training are paying off. When your life is on the line and you absolutely trust the Marines around you, that's unity."

Now that Adam's out of the Marines, there are a thousand things he doesn't miss—and one thing he wishes he could find in the civilian world.

"That unity—I don't see it," says Adam.

"Maybe it doesn't come until you've gone through things together, until you've faced danger together."

Which raises a gritty question: Since Adam is a follower of Jesus, shouldn't he be experiencing that sort of unity with other believers? What does it say that he hasn't had that experience? that unity—real unity—is so hard to find even among those of us who are together at the feet of Jesus?

Ask Jesus.

He'll tell you.

You're following, right? That's what disciples do, so there's not much for you to plan.

Just keep your eyes on Jesus and do your best to keep up.

Bless you on your journey.

PARABLE OF THE PEARL

**This letter recently washed ashore near the
oyster beds just offshore from Apalachicola, Florida...
and perhaps not by accident.**

To whatever human finds this,

Maybe you've heard it, too: "Oysters don't feel pain."

Well, as an oyster myself, I'm here to tell you otherwise.

Because we oysters don't have a centrally located brain, people
in lab coats decided we can't experience sensations like pain.
They've run tests and written stuff in notebooks and published
papers, but have they actually asked an oyster if it hurts when they
poke us?

No. They haven't.

At least, they haven't asked *me*.

Maybe that's why they've decided it's fine to yank our shells
apart and shove sand into the single most delicate spot on our
anatomy. A spot so...*personal*...that I can't even describe it in a
book that might be picked up by young children.

Let's just say this: If I did the same thing to *you*, you'd be calling
in the SWAT team to haul me off to prison.

So why would you do that to me and my oyster friends? Why
would you deliberately make us miserable?

Because you think pearls are pretty, that's why.

And, if you do it right, you can make us transform simple grains
of sand into luminescent pearls.

It works like this: Once you poke an irritant into that spot
where it bothers me most, I secrete a layer of nacre—you call it
mother-of-pearl—to coat the sand.

One coat never does the trick, so I keep adding layers. For years. And when you figure enough time has passed, someone yanks my shell open again and pulls out the pearl I've created.

Without so much as a thank you, I might add.

I mean, I get it: Sometimes pretty things show up after hard things happen.

But haven't you heard about diamonds? They're pretty, too, and it takes a whole *lot* of hard stuff to make them.

You take a lump of coal, shove it about a hundred miles under the surface of the earth where it's incredibly hot and there's a bazillion pounds of pressure, and then you wait for a volcano to urp the rock back to the surface so you can clean it up, slice it up, and polish it until it shines.

So if you like the pretty things that come after hard things happen, diamonds are the way to go.

Or if you want to see something *truly* beautiful that happens after hard shows up, decide to follow Jesus.

It's amazing what he'll do with you after you walk through a few hard things with him.

But please: Forget about pearls.

On behalf of all of us oysters, thank you.

Ollie

NOTES

NOTES

NOTES

NOTES

TAKE THE NEXT STEP TO GROW YOUR SPIRITUAL GRIT

ADVANCE YOUR JOURNEY INTO GREATER ENDURANCE, CHARACTER, CONFIDENCE, AND HOPE WITH RICK LAWRENCE'S BOOK *SPIRITUAL GRIT.*

Spiritual Grit includes:

- Ways to access the strength needed to live a resilient life through a greater dependence on Jesus.
- Biblical stories of those who grew a "grit backbone" through their interactions with Jesus.
- An extensive menu of life habits that fertilize grit, plus a method for identifying habits that undermine it.
- A way to assess your own spiritual grit.

Without Jesus, grit is little more than a gimmick. With Jesus, grit can infuse the world—and our lives—with hope.

Available now at Christian retailers and SpiritualGritBook.com.